SOCIAL MEDIA
Field Guide
2nd Edition

by Krista Neher

To My Friends and Family - I couldn't have done it without you

To My Mom - The strongest and most amazing person I know

To Joe - Your support means everything to me

Special Thanks To:

Kim Quindlen, Primary editor, researcher and project manager

Kelly Quindlen, Secondary editor

Contents

CHAPTER 1
Why Social Media?

I was recently asked to make a keynote speech for a national trade show, and I asked the organizer, "What is the biggest question your group has about building their business through social media?" His response was, "They hear about social media and are interested, but they don't know where to start. Some of them have even started, but they aren't sure if it is working or if they are getting results. They know that the Yellow Pages don't work any more, but social media can be overwhelming."

Social media is too big to ignore. Facebook has over a billion users. Twitter has over half of that with 500 million. New social networks gain a mass following more quickly than ever. People are changing their behaviors and adopting new technologies quicker than ever. Google+ gained over 30 million users in their first month.

Businesses can't afford to sit back with a "wait and see" policy. They must become adaptive and adopt new technologies at the same rate that their customers do.

The bottom line is that if you want to stay relevant with your customers, suppliers, employees and business partners, you need to participate in social media. Fish where the fish are.

This is a common problem for small business owners and large multinational companies when looking at social media. If you are new to social media, there is a lot to grasp. That is why I wrote this book – to help businesses understand the social media landscape and how to approach it strategically.

Many businesses struggle with social media because they approach it tactically without any real plan. They start by thinking "I really need to get on Facebook" instead of with a strategic objective. They start by wanting a Twitter account or Facebook page, rather than beginning with a clear understanding of their marketing objectives. Like any form of marketing, a strong strategic plan is required for success.

The best social media marketing starts with "What is my goal?" and ends with achieving it. Today 88% of businesses are on social media, but most of them are not able to quantify if or how their social media efforts have helped their business. This is the problem that this book will solve. This book is your guide to building a social media strategy and using social media tools in a strategic way that gets real results.

Social networks are becoming increasingly cluttered, making them more challenging marketing vehicles. For example, an average person on Facebook is connected to over 200 people, groups, pages and events. If each of these things posts 5 times a day, that is over 1,000 status updates that a person could be exposed to in only one day! In order to break through the noise and clutter, businesses must have a clear business and content strategy.

This book is divided into two core sections to develop a strong social media marketing strategy: The Social Media Map and the Social Media Field Guide. The Social Media Map lays the foundation for engaging in social media and includes your marketing strategy and objectives, your target audience and the rules of social media. The Social Media Field Guide is your guide to get to where you want to be on the map. By creating a great content plan and choosing the right directions and social media tools, you will be able to successfully navigate to your marketing goals and objectives.

Social Media Shouldn't Be Overwhelming

Social Media can seem overwhelming at times – there are countless social networking sites, tools that can be used to manage these social networking sites, tools for the tools…and all of these things change all the time!

The reality is that it isn't that complex, and it doesn't really change that fast. I've been doing social media marketing since its inception, and the reality is that the strategies I used 6 years ago still work today. The thing that doesn't change is the people that you are trying to reach.

While reading this book you'll learn how to build a social media strategy that transcends specific social networks. You'll learn how to create a sustainable business strategy that communicates with your customers when, where and how they are most receptive to your message.

What Is Social Media?

According to Wikipedia[1] (a social media site):

> **Social media** are media for social interaction, using highly accessible and scalable publishing techniques. Social media use web-based technologies to transform and broadcast media monologues into social media dialogues. They support the democratization of knowledge and information and transform people from content consumers to content producers. Businesses also refer to social media as user-generated content (UGC). A common thread running through all definitions of social media is a blending of technology and social interaction for the co-creation of value.
>
> Social media have become appealing to big and small businesses. Credible brands are utilizing social media to reach

---

1   http://en.wikipedia.org/wiki/Social_media

customers and to build or maintain reputation. Social media have become the new "tool" for effective business marketing and sales. Popular networking sites including MySpace, Facebook and Twitter are social media most commonly used for socialization and connecting friends, relatives, and employees.

This is a pretty lengthy definition that can be distilled to a few key points:

- It is based on social interactions, connections and conversations. It is how we connect with other people.

- It is about the combination of socializations and enabling technologies.

- Everyone has a voice and everyone can be a publisher or content creator.

- Businesses are using social media to reach consumers in many different ways.

Social media = social + media. The social part isn't new. We have been social people forever. Word of mouth marketing has been around forever. The "media" part is the variable in this equation. Now, social interactions are public and can reach large audiences.

Social media amplifies word of mouth and existing conversations.

Before "social media," most people had a small circle that they interacted with on a regular basis. Today, we can interact with hundreds or thousands of people on Twitter, Facebook and LinkedIn. In just a minute, I can post a message on Twitter that will reach over 15,000 people who follow me. Maybe some of the people who follow me will also talk about it, making the "reach" of my message even bigger. The Tweet is also public, so anyone can see it. This is the real power of social media – the ability for messages to reach many people in a transparent way.

Businesses have the opportunity to participate in and shape these messages. They can build strategies to encourage their customers to share positive experiences and build deeper emotional connections that drive loyalty.

The 7 Myths of Social Media Marketing

Social media is one of the best ways that businesses can build awareness, generate leads, drive sales, build relationships and satisfy their customers. Through my coaching and training programs, I work with thousands of business owners, and there are some common myths that I have encountered regarding social media marketing.

As a starting point, I want to remove any barriers, misconceptions or myths about social media with these 7 myths of social media marketing.

SOCIAL MEDIA MYTH #1:
Social Media Is Just a Fad

Yes, there are still people who believe that social media is still a fad and that if they ignore it long enough it will go away. You clearly are not one of them since you made the smart choice to read this book.

The reality is that social media is built on age-old concepts of socializing, communities and word-of-mouth marketing. It isn't a fad. While you may not be using social networks yourself, there is no denying that the vast majority of the global population is.

The underlying premise of social media – that people are social and want to connect with other people – has been stable over time. What is different is that we are now able to connect with people in a more efficient and scalable way. Through Facebook, you can see what friends from high school are up to without ever speaking to them. You can see photos of friends and family across the world by looking at their photos. You can see where your neighbors are going for drinks and what they thought of the play they saw last night. Social media allows people to keep up to speed with many people in quick and efficient ways.

The point? Social media isn't going away, because our need to socialize and the media of the Internet aren't going away any time soon. Rather than focusing on the latest and greatest site people are buzzing about, focus on the core trends and behaviors – these don't change much. My Social

Marketing Success Method is based on building a marketing strategy that is timeless and not based around single tools that change over time.

Social media marketing is also in some ways a new form of word-of-mouth marketing. We have always shared our consumer experiences with our friends – told them about the amazing food at a new restaurant or the horrible customer service we had while furniture shopping. The difference is that these conversations are now happening online, and they are happening on a larger scale than ever before.

Still not convinced? The numbers speak for themselves.

- Facebook now has over 1 billion users. That is bigger than the populations of the United States, Canada and Mexico combined[2].

- YouTube has 1 billion unique monthly users[3].

- There are 1.3 billion smart phone app downloads each day on Apple and Android[4].

- In the first quarter of 2010 online spending grew 10% to almost $34 billion[5].

- According to Comscore metrics, social media sites are experiencing a 50% growth in traffic year over year[6].

- 2 million blog posts are published every day.[7]

- Social media drives decision-making. When looking for purchase information, US adults look first to search, then to blogs, user-generated media, message boards and social networks. Traditional media—magazines, TV and newspapers— ranks at the bottom[8].

---

2   http://www.facebook.com/press.php#!/press/info.php?statistics

3   http://youtube-global.blogspot.com/2013/03/onebillionstrong.html

4   http://www.brandwatch.com/2013/02/look-guys-incredible-social-media-statistics/

5   http://www.comscore.com/Press_Events/Press_Releases/2010/5/comScore_
    Reports_Q1_2010_U.S._E-Commerce_Spending_Accelerates_to_a_10_Percent_
    Growth_vs._Year_Ago

6   http://comscore.com – March 2010 compared to March 2009

7   http://www.brandwatch.com/2013/02/look-guys-incredible-social-media-statistics/

8   http://www.scribd.com/doc/31277666/
    BlogHer-iVillage-2010-Social-Media-Matters-Study

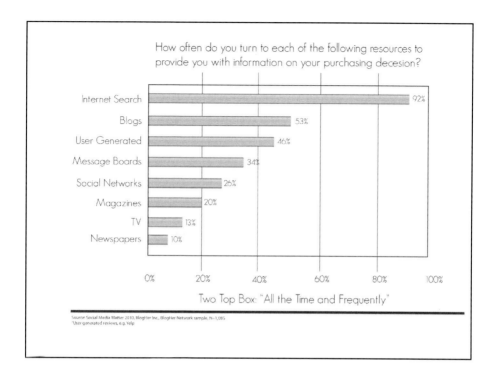

How often do you turn to each of the following resources to provide you with information on your purchasing decesion?

Resource	Percentage
Internet Search	92%
Blogs	53%
User Generated	46%
Message Boards	34%
Social Networks	26%
Magazines	20%
TV	13%
Newspapers	10%

Two Top Box: "All the Time and Frequently"

Source: Social Media Matter 2010, BlogHer Inc., BlogHer Network sample, N=1,085
*User generated reviews, e.g. Yelp

SOCIAL MEDIA MYTH #2:
Social Media Is Just for the Young

Many social media skeptics think that social media is a tool primarily for the young: kids, teenagers and college students. The reality is that social media is used widely by all age groups.

- YouTube reports that their user base is broad in age range, 18-55, evenly divided between males and females, and spanning all geographies[9].

- People over 65 are adopting Facebook quicker than any other group[10].

- 48% of people over 55 have Facebook accounts[11].

---

9   http://www.youtube.com

10 http://www.nytimes.com/2010/07/18/technology/18death.
    html?_r=1&scp=6&sq=facebook&st=cse

11 http://www.morpace.com/Omnibus-Reports/Omnibus%20Report-
    Facebooks%20Impact%20on%20Retailers.pdf

- 32% of people aged 65 and older now use social networking sites. [12]

- 10% of people aged 30-49 now use Twitter. [13]

Social networks are increasingly being adopted by older populations and are becoming incredibly diverse – spanning all age and income brackets.

When it comes to social media marketing, many organizations think that an intern or new college graduate is the best person to run their social media. The reality is that young people or "digital natives" know how social networks operate and are accustomed to using them to socialize; however, they aren't necessarily well equipped to build and execute social media marketing strategies.

The strategic part of social media requires marketing knowledge and strategic thinking. This is where experienced and seasoned marketers play a key role in social media. Social media marketing, like any type of marketing, requires strategic thinking and a deep understanding of your core consumers. These are not skills that are typically seen in interns and new graduates. While younger people may make great executors due to their innate understanding of how the social networks operate, they are probably not the best strategic marketers.

You wouldn't hire the person who watches the most TV to "do your TV." They would make a good focus group at best. The same is true with social media marketing. While the field is new and there aren't a lot of experienced people out there, sound marketing strategies are vital to the success of your social media marketing campaign.

SOCIAL MEDIA MYTH #3:
There Is No Return in Social Media Marketing

I could write an entire book on this topic alone. As social media marketing has continued to grow and evolve, more studies have emerged that

---

12 http://www.pewinternet.org/Reports/2013/Social-media-users/Social-Networking-Site-Users/Overview.aspx

13 http://www.pewinternet.org/Reports/2013/Social-media-users/Social-Networking-Site-Users/Demo-portrait.aspx

highlight the return on investment (ROI) and traceable value of social media marketing.

Some examples of how social media drives ROI include:

- Pinterest has been shown to drive purchasers to websites, and people who go to a website from Pinterest are 10% more likely to buy and spend 10% more on average. [14]

- 73% of shoppers said that Facebook influenced a recent store visit.[15]

- 75% of consumers talk about brands on Facebook.

- 66% of consumers have already made a purchase based on social content. [16]

- 34% of marketers have generated leads from Twitter. [17]

- 54% of consumers share their purchases socially on Facebook, Twitter, Pinterest, and other social sites. [18]

While ROI (return on investment) is a specific monetary value determined by an established method, social media return is measured in a variety of different ways and not always as clear-cut. A strategic social media campaign can be measured and the specific sources of value can be determined.

Many businesses are seeing actual measurable returns through their social media marketing efforts.

- Dell generated $6.5 million dollars from their Twitter account.

- Marriott got over $500 million in bookings directly from their blog.

---

14 http://pinnablebusiness.com/
study-finds-at-least-20-have-purchased-product-seen-on-sites-like-pinterest/

15 http://www.empathica.com/
infographic-us-consumer-usage-of-social-media-to-make-shopping-decisions/

16 http://www.massrelevance.com/press-release/mass-relevance-releases-new-research-social-integration-drives-consumer-engagement#.UVTJCls4VR4

17 http://www.mediabistro.com/alltwitter/digital-marketing-2011_b15395

18 http://www.grabstats.com/statmain.aspx?StatID=1485

- Golden Tee saved tens of thousands of dollars running a contest on Facebook.

- VistaPrints sold $30 thousand from social media marketing.

- Lenovo saved costs with a 20% reduction in customer service calls by using social media.

- Naked Pizza, a small regional pizza chain, had their highest-ever sales day from deals posted on Twitter.

- Adobe ran contests on Facebook and Twitter that led to 83,000 social conversations and 97% positive-neutral statements in 5 days. [19]

These case studies highlight the actual tangible dollar return from companies of all sizes using social media. Both small, independent retailers and large, multi-national companies have seen success from social media marketing. Both business-to-business and business-to-consumer companies are generating value from social media.

In addition to direct attributable sales, a number of less measurable benefits arise from social media marketing. Customer service savings, development cost savings from using open platforms, positive equity build, awareness, lead generation, email opt-ins - the list could go on and on.

SOCIAL MEDIA MYTH #4:
Social Media Marketing Isn't Right for my Fill-in-the-Blank Business

If human beings are purchasing your product or making purchase decisions, then social media is right for your business. Many B-to-B companies question whether social media makes sense for them. The answer is YES because:

1) People are on social media and they spend LOTS of time on it.

2) People want to connect with brands on social media in a relevant way.

---

19 http://econsultancy.com/us/blog/62217-five-examples-of-b2b-companies-achieving-success-in-social-marketing

3) Some types of businesses think that social media doesn't apply to them, so it is a way to get an edge on the competition.

For almost any business, there are opportunities in social media simply because the people you are trying to reach are active on it. A third of US adults are frequent social media users – and that number is growing.

Why do businesses market on television, in magazines and on billboards? Because that is where their audience is. Marketers connect with people where they spend their time and, increasingly, that time is being spent on social media.

In addition to time shifting towards social media, the reality is that people want to interact with brands on social media. According to Facebook[20], an average Facebooker is connected to over 80 brand pages, community pages and events. A recent Morpace study[21] found that people join fan pages primarily to let their friends know the products they like (word-of-mouth) and to receive coupons and discounts (direct sales opportunity).

Social media is also powerful for its ability to drive word-of-mouth or recommendations from friends – 57% of Facebookers state that they use Facebook to discuss products and services with friends and nearly 68% of consumers say that a positive referral from a friend on Facebook makes them more likely to buy a specific product or visit a certain retailer.

Regardless of your business type, people are searching for your brand, product or business online for information to help guide their purchase (there are almost 25 billion online searches each month[22]). Search is the #1 resource used when looking for information about a product online, with 92% of people using it. Social media relates to search as a resource because search results often include social media sites. Facebook, LinkedIn, Wikipedia, Yelp, Yahoo!Answers, Review Sites, Blogs and other social media sites consistently show up on the first page of search results.

Even if you don't believe in the value of engaging in social conversations as a part of your marketing, there is no denying the value of your

---

20 http://www.facebook.com/press.php#!/press/info.php?statistics

21 http://www.morpace.com/Omnibus-Reports/Omnibus%20Report-Facebooks%20Impact%20on%20Retailers.pdf

22 http://www.comscore.com/Press_Events/Press_Releases/2010/7/comScore_Releases_June_2010_U.S._Search_Engine_Rankings

business or product showing up in search results. If you are not managing and monitoring social media, you may be surprised by what shows up. A search for "Comcast" returns a video of a Comcast technician falling asleep on a customer's sofa while on hold with Comcast customer service. This video, posted in 2006, is still a first page Google search result for Comcast.

In addition to search, the shift in consumer attention from traditional media to online media is reason enough to use social media. Many businesses are used to marketing through television, radio, newspapers, yellow pages or direct mail like ValPak. These methods are becoming obsolete. People are watching less traditional TV and are watching videos online through YouTube and television shows online through sites like Hulu.com. I cancelled my cable years ago and now watch all of my favorite shows on demand through Hulu.com or on ABC.com or CBS.com. Radio is being replaced by online streaming of customized music on sites like Pandora. com or Slacker.com. Newspapers are in dramatic decline with more going out of business each day, while blogs are growing in popularity. The Yellow Pages are more likely to be used to hold up a computer monitor than to locate a business. ValPak coupons end up in the garbage since the same coupons can be found online when the consumer actually needs them.

Stop wasting your money on dying media and invest in a marketing method that is growing quickly and showing returns.

SOCIAL MEDIA MYTH #5:
Social Media Marketing is Mostly About What We Post

I believe that one of the biggest pieces of value that brands or businesses can get from social media is in driving word of mouth.

- 60% of consumers reported that they were more likely to share experiences with a brand or product that incorporates social media on their website.

- 65% of consumers who use social media to interact with brands have purchased a product based on social media content.

- 63% of consumers are more likely to buy new products or try new things based on social content.[23]

Why is social media so valuable at driving word of mouth? Because we are connected to people like us. This is known as the social graph, which is basically how we are all connected to one another. **This means that our best next customers are the people who are connected to our current customers on social networks.**

Using social media to get your current customers talking is a great way to drive value. Businesses often view social media as a place for them to post content on their page, and to try to grow likes of their page. Social media is an ecosystem where people are all connected to one another.

Don't miss the bigger opportunities of social media to recommend, connect and drive visibility for your business with their friends and connections. Look at social networks as an ecosystem and explore how you can build relationships and encourage your current customers, business partners and other organizations to help you spread the word.

SOCIAL MEDIA MYTH #6:
Social Media Is Too Time-Consuming

Many businesses' owners and individuals think social media marketing is too time-consuming. Typically, this is because they aren't working smart or haven't invested the time to understand how to get the best results.

Once your social media profiles are set up, you can effectively manage your social media assets and get results with just 15 minutes, 5 days a week, which is just an hour and 15 minutes total per week (depending on the size and nature of your business). Even the busiest people can fit that into their schedule.

For example, if you are already reading relevant industry news, it only takes a minute to share the best news with your thoughts on Facebook or Twitter. If you are active in your business, it only takes a moment to snap a picture to share on Instagram or Pinterest. Social Media doesn't have to be a separate business process; it can be integrated into the activities that you are already involved with.

---

23 http://www.massrelevance.com/press-release/mass-relevance-releases-new-research-social-integration-drives-consumer-engagement#.UVTJCls4VR4

In our Social Media Marketing Training Programs, we've created a clear method for how companies can get results with this small time investment, and it works. Social media doesn't have to be time-consuming when done right. The problem is that many people log on to Facebook, Twitter or LinkedIn and get sucked in to checking out what all their friends are up to. Or they end up checking these sites multiple times a day.

There are three key ways to limit the time investment in social media marketing:

1) The first is to look for underutilized resources that can spend some of their time on social media marketing. For example, I did a social media consultation with a gym and the owner told me that he didn't have time to manage social media. I pointed out that the people behind the desk were only actually busy and working a small percentage of the time. If he could train them to manage his social media assets, he could actually get more out of his employees without increasing his costs. The fact is that you don't have to do everything yourself.

2) The second opportunity is to leverage efficiency tools. There are a number of sites, like HootSuite, TweetDeck and CoTweet, which make managing social media easier. By using these tools, you can accomplish more in less time.

3) Finally, leveraging mobile devices can drive efficiency. This is especially helpful for publishing photos and videos. From my smart phone (like a Blackberry, iPhone or Android phone), I can take a picture or video and instantly post it onto my Facebook page in under a minute. This makes social media management even easier and less time-consuming.

SOCIAL MEDIA MYTH #7:
Social Media Is Free

Many businesses are excited about social media because they see it as free marketing. While most sites don't have a fee to use them, social media isn't really free. First, there is the cost in terms of time, resources and possibly consultants or agencies involved in building and executing the social media strategy. Social media takes time, and that alone means it is not free.

Second, similar to other media and advertising, in addition to just posting the content there may be costs to produce and create the content. Imagine if it was free to run TV commercials – companies didn't have to pay for time on TV networks. There would be LOTS of commercials – and many terrible ones that don't drive results. Free means no barrier to entry. Good commercials would still have costs for creative and production. In a similar way, strong social media strategies often include creative or development costs depending on their scale.

Finally, many businesses engaging in social media invest in tools, training or agencies to support their efforts. Many of the most successful businesses invest in the tools and training that will get them better results faster.

Why Social Media Marketing Is Different

Voices Are Amplified

In the age of social media, consumer voices are amplified. Consumers talking about brands, products and businesses is not new – we have done this forever. What is new is that the voices of average people are amplified. Through social media an average person can make a comment that is seen by hundreds, thousands or even millions of people. For example, I have over 15,000 people who follow me on Twitter. This means that when I have a bad or good experience with a business, I can reach over 15,000 people with just a few keystrokes.

This is one of the main reasons that companies are taking note of social media. It isn't just the traditional press that can reach large audiences – everyone can. Everyone has the potential to reach large audiences and even the traditional press is finding stories from social media. Since average people have the opportunity to reach such large audiences, it is more important than ever to manage their opinions of your brand.

More Transparency

Social media leads to a more transparent marketplace. Information is more readily available. Through review sites and customer ratings, consumers can talk to each other and learn from each other faster than ever before.

Think about the last time you made an online purchase, maybe from a site like Amazon.com. One of the first things most people look at before making a purchase is the star rating of a product. In fact, consumers are willing to pay 20% - 99% more for a product that has a 5-star rating versus a product with a 4-star rating.

According to a Nielsen study about trust in advertising, people trust recommendations from people they know and people they don't know (consumer opinions posted online). They also trust many online assets like websites and emails more than they trust advertising. This means that

To what extent do you trust the following forms of advertising?		
Global Average	Trust Completely/ Somewhat	Don't Trust Much/ At All
Recommendations from people I know	92%	8%
Consumer opinions posted online	70%	30%
Editorial content such as newspaper articles	58%	42%
Branded Websites	58%	42%
Emails I signed up for	50%	50%
Ads on TV	47%	53%
Brand sponsorships	47%	53%
Ads in magazines	47%	53%
Billboards and other outdoor advertising	47%	53%
Ads in newspapers	46%	54%
Ads on radio	42%	58%
Ads before movies	41%	59%
TV program product placements	40%	60%
Ads served in search engine results	40%	60%
Online video ads	36%	64%
Ads on social networks	36%	64%
Online banner ads	33%	67%
Display ads on mobile devices	33%	67%
Text ads on mobile phones	29%	71%

Source: Nielsen Global Trust in Advertising Survey, Q3 2011

social media that drives recommendations and reviews can be powerful at influencing behavior because it is highly trusted.

Brand advertising has less of an impact on what influences our purchases, and consumers, people like us, sharing their experiences and opinions have a greater influence.

If there is a problem or issue with your product or customer service, chances are people will find out - quickly. Through social media, consumers can connect with each other almost immediately. Your problems and issues will become public, and it is vital that you have a plan to address these issues and respond to consumers in a helpful and transparent way.

One of my CEO coaching clients told me that he was concerned that if they built a social media presence, their customers might say bad things about them. They were in the financial services business, and they had a big problem with their customers understanding some of the complexities of their policies. We did a quick search and found that people were already saying bad things about their policies on blogs, discussion forums and Twitter. The conversations were already taking place – people were already saying bad things. The problem with *not* having a social media presence is that their company didn't have the opportunity to respond. Most of the complaints stemmed from misunderstandings of the policies. By getting active on social media, the company would have the opportunity to respond and help clarify the policies and why they were in place.

Brands and companies need to monitor the social media space to know what people are saying about them so that they can respond appropriately. As they say in *GI Joe*, "Knowing is half the battle."

Social Media Is Conversations

Many companies have trouble with social media because social media is about conversations between actual people. It is personal and conversational. For businesses to succeed, they too must be personal and conversational.

People on social media are not looking to be overtly advertised or marketed to. They are looking to connect with their friends and family and talk about their interests. Brands can be a part of this, but they have to be conversational and relevant – not obtrusive.

Part of the reason brands struggle with social media is because they can't resist the urge to sell and they don't see the opportunities for subtle marketing.

For example, a friend of mine owns a company that sells promotional products like customized T-shirts, pens, trade show items, etc. He is very active on Twitter and primarily talks about marketing and general social topics. He periodically mentions new products his business is carrying or shares information about an affiliate program. When he shares this information, it is in a personal way, for example "I'm so excited about the new T-shirt line we are carrying – what do you think?" and includes a URL to a photo of him wearing the shirt. Without saying, "HEY – I SELL SHIRTS. COME AND BUY THEM," he is able to get across the message in a way that appeals to the audience.

The key for brands wishing to connect with people on social media is to engage in the conversation that is actually taking place. Forget about talking about your brand and overtly selling; just join the conversation. This sounds easy, but time and again brands try to shift the conversation back to themselves instead of just participating in the conversation that is happening.

Overt selling and marketing is a turn-off for most people in social media – unless it is high-value and requested. For example, many people choose to follow the Dell Outlet Twitter account to get great deals on Dell products. People who follow Dell Outlet know exactly what they are getting (deals and offers). The Dell Outlet account doesn't pretend to be conversational – they are just selling (although Dell does have other accounts that offer customer service). The key to directly selling on social media is to be open and transparent about it. Don't pretend to be conversational and then spam people with sales offers. Be open about your intentions.

Social Media and Traditional Marketing Work Together

Marketing is connected. Channels do not operate in isolation. All of your marketing efforts both online and offline work together to influence consumer behavior, and they should be consistent.

For example, my company is a member of the Better Business Bureau (and they are now a client). I had always known of the Better Business Bureau (BBB), but hadn't thought about joining. In researching competitors one day, I noticed that many of them had their BBB accreditation on their websites, and it got me thinking about joining. I went to the website but wasn't ready to make a decision, but it was on my radar as a tool that could help grow my business.

A few weeks later I was at an advertising event that they sponsored, and I was exposed to the BBB again, and once again thought about joining. A few weeks later I saw an interesting article about scams from the BBB on Facebook. I liked the article and the BBB on Facebook, but still hadn't joined.

A few weeks after that, I got a call from a BBB sales rep, and I joined the BBB. If the BBB is measuring the effectiveness of their marketing, they may credit that sale to their direct sales team (the people who called me). In reality it was all of the touch points together that ultimately caused me to sign up.

The fact that the BBB was a brand that I already had heard of, knew, and trusted was a big part of the picture. Seeing it on competitive sites made me actually want to join, and exposure to events that they sponsored and Facebook posts built my trust. The call closed the deal, but without the other elements it wouldn't have happened.

Social media isn't a stand-alone platform. All marketing is connected and multiple touch points are often required to convert a customer. This is why traditional marketers use television, radio and print and expose each person to multiple ads. It takes more than a single interaction to close a sale.

ACTION ITEMS AND KEY LEARNINGS

Want to put the Social Media Field Guide into Action?
Go to **www.bootcampdigital.com/actionplanner** to
download your FREE Field Guide action planner.

ACTION ITEMS AND KEY LEARNINGS

Want to put the Social Media Field Guide into Action?
Go to www.bootcampdigital.com/actionplanner to
download your FREE Field Guide action planner.

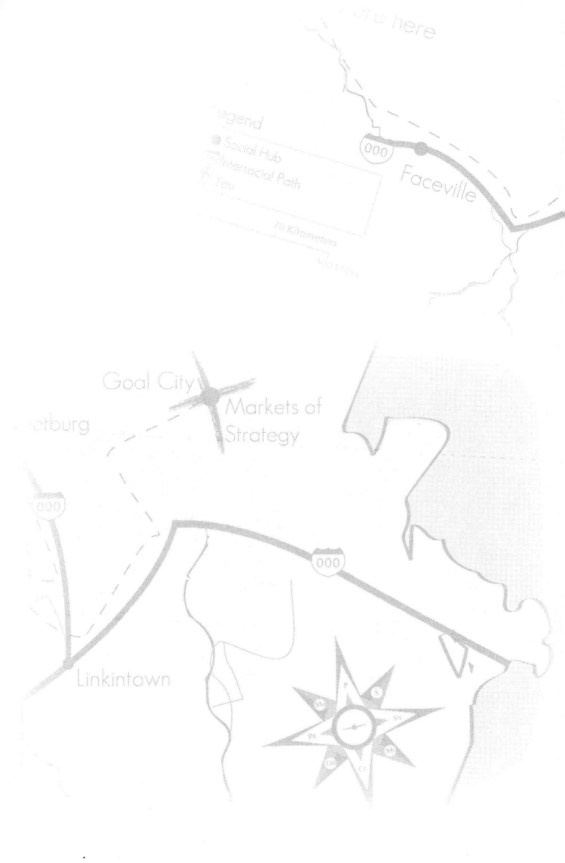

PART 1:
Building Your Social Media Plan

The Social Media Map

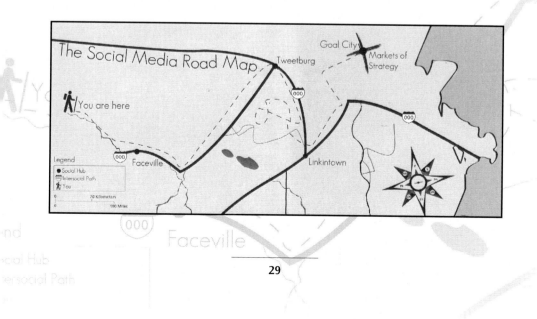

CHAPTER 2:

Strategy and Objectives –
The Destination

- - - - - - - - - - - - - -

The Social Media Map will help you successfully navigate social media and get from where you are right now to your desired end point – much like a road map. The end point is your marketing goals and objectives. Prior to getting started in social media marketing, it is important to know where you want to end up. What do you want to achieve? This is your strategies and objectives.

Having a clear strategy is key to success in social media – without a clearly defined strategy, it is difficult to set goals and objectives, execute social media strategically and ultimately measure success. Defining your objectives will also help you to determine how to build a Call to Action into your social media marketing strategy. From here, you can actively track, measure and adjust your social media strategy.

Understanding your goals and objectives is the starting point for social media marketing. Many businesses "get on social media" without a clear idea of what they want to achieve. They post random updates that are largely ignored and don't grow the business.

I've consulted with hundreds of businesses, and the #1 mistake that businesses make on social media is not defining their goals upfront. Clear goals lead to a strategic execution that adds value, which leads to a clearly measurable plan.

Building a Social Media Plan – The Social Marketing System

Building and executing your social media plan is a continuous process that both starts and finishes with listening and observing. Most companies that are successful with social media are constantly testing new things and adjusting their strategies based on what they learn. It is important to think about all of these steps in your social media plan-building and work processes.

After training thousands of people and working with hundreds of companies I realized that the biggest problem that companies have is approaching social media strategically. The Social Marketing System is a step-by-step method to developing a solid social media marketing plan that gets real results. This system has been successfully used by many different businesses and is also at the core of the textbook I coauthored on social media marketing.

An advertising agency that attended one of my Boot Camp Training sessions used this system to win their first social media marketing work (and it was a 6 figure contract!). I worked with a small business owner on this who was able to build an engaging social strategy and generate thousands of connections in only a week!

Listen and Observe -> Define your Strategy -> Identify your Target Audience -> Content -> Select the Tools -> Execute ->Measure and Monitor ->Evaluate and Improve ->

The Social Marketing System matches how this book is structured. The first section is Listening, Marketing Strategies and Target Audience in Chapters 2, 3 and 4. The Social Media Field Guide covers Content and Tools and provides some guidance around implementation and execution. From there you will need to build tracking and measuring tools into your marketing plans so you can continuously adjust and improve your strategies.

LISTEN AND OBSERVE:
5 Things to Listen to

Before jumping in to social media, it is important to listen and observe both your target audience as well as the social media landscape in general. During the listen and observe stage, you want to listen to conversations about your brand and company, your competitors, your industry and different channels. You also want to listen for the overall tone of the community.

#1: Listen to Conversations about Your Brand or Company

The first stage of listening is listening to and observing conversations about your brand and your company. What are people saying about your brand? What are the good and bad things being said? How do people feel about your company?

Listen to the conversations taking place on blogs, Twitter, Pinterest, discussion forums, websites, LinkedIn, Facebook, etc., to understand how you are perceived. This will help you understand where your opportunities lie. In addition, understanding what consumers are already saying about you will help you prepare responses for common questions or issues. It can help you anticipate areas that you should be prepared to address when you become active in social media.

#2: Listen to What People Say about Your Competitors

Next, listen to what people are saying about your competitors and what your competitors are saying about themselves. What do people say about your competitors in the social space? What are the pros and cons? How might this impact your business? Are there opportunities for you?

In addition to listening to how people feel about your competitors, it is helpful to identify the competitive social media landscape. What are your competitors doing on social media? Who are they targeting? What seems to work? What doesn't work? What can you learn from them? How can you approach this better than they are?

Assessing the competitive landscape on social media sites will help you see how people are connecting with competitors and may provide you with insights that you can leverage when building your strategy.

#3: Listening to What People Say about Your Industry or Category

After observing your competition, take your listening up a notch to the industry. What are consumers (or potential consumers or people in your target audience) saying about your industry? What is the sentiment? Does this create opportunities? What conversations do they have around the industry? What are passion points and pain points?

Developing an understanding of the conversations taking place around your industry will help you understand what people are interested in talking about. We will discuss content in Chapter 5, but one thing to keep in mind in creating social media content is to connect with consumers around something that they are passionate about (which typically isn't your brand). Listening, at the category or industry level, will help you understand what consumers are really interested in talking about in association with your industry.

#4: Listening to Different Social Media Channels

When listening in social media, be sure to listen across different social media channels. Discussions and interactions on Facebook may be dramatically different from those on Twitter, LinkedIn, Google+ or blogs. Each social media channel has a different audience and different conversations. Some social networks are anonymous while others are tied to a personal profile. Some are personal and others are professional. Since usage on each site is different, it is important to listen to conversations across a variety of social media channels.

#5: Listening to Your Target

The final stage of listening is to listen to and really get to understand your target audience. Find a handful of people that represent the audience you want to reach. What lingo and tone do they use? How do they interact with each other? What are the words that they naturally use to describe their feelings around your brand, competitors or industry? What else do they talk about? What is on their mind? What are the unwritten rules of participation? Who is getting attention? Who are the influencers? How do they talk and what are they interested in?

When you engage in social media you want to fit in and sound like your consumers. You also want to understand them as complete people, not just in how they interact with your product. It is important to first develop an understanding of how they communicate with each other and the etiquette of communicating on different social sites so you can easily integrate and participate in the community.

Listening and observing is the key first step in the social media planning stage. Spending time observing will help you with the rest of the social media strategy planning process.

Defining Your Strategy & Objectives

Defining your marketing objectives is a key step in building a strong social media marketing plan (or any marketing plan for that matter). Different marketing goals and objectives will lend themselves to different social media executions. The key in defining your marketing objectives is to understand what you want to achieve with social media. What is your desired outcome?

Keep in mind that while you may set out with a specific set of goals and objectives in mind, it is important to be flexible as you may discover unintended benefits from social media engagement. For example, I interviewed Jeff Esposito, who runs social media at Vista Prints. Jeff told me that after Vista Prints got started on Twitter they realized that many people were looking for customer service support on Twitter. Rather than refusing to respond to customer service inquiries, Jeff engaged the customer service department and created a process where they were notified of customer service questions and responded directly to the tweets.

According to the 2012 Social Media Marketing Industry Report, brands are using social media in some unexpected ways. The first few are obvious – 85% of all marketers use it to generate more exposure for their business, 69% use it to increase traffic, and 58% use it to generate leads. What is surprising is some of the other uses of social media. 51% use it to grow business partnerships, 46% use it to reduce marketing expenses, and 40% use it to improve sales. Many of these uses are unexpected benefits to social media. I'm sure that most brands set out with a different objective in terms of how they would use social media. It is important to keep an open mind and be flexible in your social media plans.

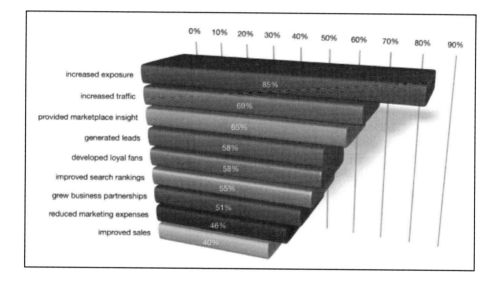

Social Media Marketing Strategies

Marketing objectives and strategies may include (but are not limited to):

- **Building awareness** – One of the top priorities for many businesses is often to build general awareness for the product or service being offered. This is true for large brands and individuals because Marketing 101 tells us that the more familiar someone is with a brand, the more likely they are to buy it. For example, insurance agents and real estate agents do a lot of networking just to build awareness of their services. They know that you might not need their services right now, but they want to be the first person that comes to mind when you need something. In this case, their goal is to build awareness with as many people as possible. Consumer goods like laundry detergent or potato chips may initially aim to increase general awareness for their brand or new product.

- **Building brand equity/positioning** – If people already know your brand, you may have an opportunity to create a more positive image or attach a more specific attribute to the impression that people have of your product. For example, if you are Tide laundry detergent, most people know of the brand; however, there may be equity-building opportunities, so that people associate "the best clean" or "the best smell" with Tide. If you are in a competitive industry (and we all are) you need to position yourself differently from your competition. A coffee shop might want to be known for serving the best quality coffee, for providing the best place to work or for offering the freshest baked goods.

- **Developing brand equity as the experts** – Position your brand or company as thought leaders and experts in your industry by showcasing your unique knowledge is often the goal of social media (especially to B-to-B). If company X knows more about the subject area than anyone else, they *must* be creating high-quality products. A thought leadership strategy involves creating content that highlights your unique expertise in a subject area.

- **Attracting new customers** – Social media can help businesses to acquire new customers. This can be done passively – by sharing great content – or actively – by running deals and promotions or directly responding to information requests.

- **Increasing search engine ranking** – Search engines, like Google, have a number of factors that impact where your website shows up when people search for a specific topic. A blog can improve your search engine ranking because blogs are content rich and use lots of key words. Producing blogs, videos, e-books and white papers can help make your website visible when people search for key terms associated with your company, product and industry. Additionally, social media profiles on sites like Twitter, LinkedIn and Facebook often show up towards the top of search engine results.

- **Establishing trust** – Companies can establish trust with consumers by displaying their knowledge of a product area and their genuine interest in the topics that their customers are interested in. Publishing web content allows companies to show a more personal side to their executives and organization. This means they can explain policies and practices and share news in a more human and conversational voice. Additionally, by honestly and openly engaging in conversations, brands can further build trust, which can ultimately earn sales.

- **Generating leads** – Social media can also be a great strategy for generating leads – especially if you can create content that requires an email address to register. E-books, white papers and webinars are all publishing tools that typically require someone to enter their email address to receive your free content. In addition to collecting an email address, a brief survey prior to downloading the content can be used to qualify leads for sales teams. Attaining an email address creates the opportunity to send marketing messages (newsletters, special offers, etc.) over a lifetime (provided they don't unsubscribe).

- **Selling your product** – When appropriate, you can publish or share content to sell your product directly. Zappos, an online company that sells shoes, clothes and makeup, has a number of blogs, but their Fashion blog directly makes recommendations about trendy styles and provides direct links to their products. They talk directly about their products, but they provide helpful information about how they can be used. Additionally, producing tutorials or information on how your product is used can drive sales. For example, a semi-professional photography lighting company can create videos on how to use lighting in different photography settings using their products. The goal is to showcase the product and drive sales. This strategy can also increase loyalty since existing customers can enhance their experience with your products as well. Vista prints, an online printing company, generated over $30,000 in sales directly from promotions offered on Twitter and Facebook.

- **Building relationships** – Social media is a key way to build relationships. Building relationships is important because people do business with people they know, like and trust. By engaging in social media with a human element, brands have the opportunity to build real relationships with their target audiences.

- **Providing customer service** – Many companies are using social media for customer service. Twitter is a popular tool for customer service because you can directly respond to comments or questions. Additionally, using Twitter to broadcast issues can actually cut down on customer service costs. Twitter, blogs and discussion forums also provide opportunities for customers to help each other solve issues, saving you time and money.

- **Developing new product ideas** – By listening and engaging with customers and potential customers, brands can discover new product ideas or new feature and service requests. Rather than occasionally running focus groups, by continuously listening to the social space, brands have the opportunity to learn from customers continually and use this information to improve their products and create new ones.

- **Increasing customer satisfaction** – Following up through social media channels or just being nice can have significant impacts on customer satisfaction. Social media provides the opportunity for brands to build real relationships and resolve issues that can dramatically increase customer satisfaction. Just knowing that a brand or business cares enough to listen is often enough to increase customer satisfaction.

- **Increasing customer loyalty** – For many businesses, 80% of their sales come from 20% of their customers. What if you could make more of your customers more loyal? That might be easier (and more profitable) than constantly focusing your energy on acquiring new customers. Building relationships through social media (or in real life) can increase customer loyalty.

- **Driving word-of-mouth recommendations** – Even more powerful than driving loyalty from your current customers is having them do your marketing for you by telling friends and family about your product or service. Social media is about people talking to each other. Brands and businesses that engage in the conversation are more likely to gain recommendations on social sites because they are at the top of people's minds.

- **Providing information about your product or category** – For complex purchases or most business-to-business categories, consumers are looking for information. Social media publishing tools like blogs and webinars can be powerful and easy ways to share information about your product or category.

- **Soliciting feedback from customers** – Social media can create a two-way dialogue of soliciting feedback and product ideas from customers. Blogs, podcasts and even Facebook fan pages all allow for company-consumer conversation. Many brands will poll their social media sites about new products (do you prefer red or green?) or other aspects of their business.

- **Focus groups** – Large companies spend millions of dollars every year on focus groups getting customer feedback. Instead of actively soliciting feedback, companies can simply listen to social networks to learn what consumers are saying about their products, their competitors or the category or industry. Social media conversations are unfiltered and real, so brands can learn a lot just by listening in on conversations.

- **Humanizing your brand** – Social media is a powerful way to put a human face to your brand. We do business with people we know, like and trust. By showing the human side of your business, people are more likely to know, like and trust you in return. We feel a connection with people that we rarely feel towards faceless corporations.

- **Gaining attention from industry analysts and press** – Press and industry analysts are increasingly looking to social media to build their stories. Most big, traditional publications like *The New York Times* and *The Wall Street Journal* pick up stories that start in the blogosphere. In addition, many journalists are using search engines to research their stories. If your content shows up in search engines, you may have more opportunities.

- **Better communicating corporate news** – A blog can provide a company with the opportunity to share corporate news in a way that is open and transparent in using normal human language. It can also be used to share news that does not warrant a press release.

This list of 20 potential marketing objectives and strategies is not by any means endless. These are simply some of the most common marketing objectives. An integrated marketing strategy may combine a number of these strategies, and different aspects of the social media plan may focus on different marketing objectives. It is important to initiate your social media execution with a clear idea of what you are hoping to achieve so that you can choose the content and tools that are most appropriate.

Determining Your Marketing Strategy

There are some key considerations when creating your marketing strategy and objectives.

What Are Your Overall Marketing Goals?

Look to the general marketing goals for your organization when looking to create your social media goals. Social media should not be an isolated part of your marketing strategy – it should link to your broader marketing plans. Build a social media strategy that supports the overall strategic goals for your company – this will also make it easier to win support for your social media strategy.

What Did We Learn from Listening?

During the listening stage, you should have observed conversations about your company, your competitors and your category. What did you learn from this? Where is your audience and what are they interested in speaking about? Where are your current and future customers? What do they talk about? How are your competitors using social media? What does this tell you about the strategic opportunities?

In addition to listening to your target audience, listening across different channels is also important. How are different social channels used to address different marketing goals and objectives? How can you leverage these for your organization?

What Stages of the Marketing Funnel Do We Want to Focus On?

Businesses often make the mistake of tying their social media objectives only to sales. This is a mistake because we know that people rarely buy something the first time that they hear about it. We don't see a television commercial for a fast food chain and jump off the couch to eat there immediately.

They are building awareness, interest and desire so that the next day at lunch it is the first place on our mind. Even with businesses that sell products or services online, a person visits a site an average of 5.7 times before buying. This means that marketers must understand the funnel that consumers go through that ultimately leads them to purchase, and market to all of the stages of the funnel.

Objectives May Change.
Be Flexible.

Launch with a plan, but be flexible so you can adapt and adjust once you start. The social media planning model is a fluid circle – it is flexible and adaptive. Once you gain experience in social media, you will learn and measure your results, which may lead you to change your strategy and objectives. You may change your objectives over time as you build experience in social media.

For example, you may discover that your customers want to use Twitter for customer service or that your existing customers are really active on Facebook. Be open to adapting once you jump in – you may be surprised at how social media can work in ways you may not have initially anticipated.

Linking Your Objectives to a Call to Action

Once you have clear marketing goals and objectives, it is important to link your goals and objectives to a call to action (or multiple calls to action). This will help you design and measure your social media campaigns (and all of your Internet marketing) more effectively. **In order to measure your success, you need to clearly define what exactly it was that you wanted someone to do – your call to action.** If you have a clear and measurable call to action, you can measure conversions on your site and the effectiveness of your online marketing.

A call to action is simply the action that you want someone to take. You may have different calls to action for different parts of your Internet marketing strategy or social media strategy.

For example, you may want blog readers to subscribe to your email newsletter or a webinar, but your call to action for webinar listeners may be for them to sign up for your product. To this end, you may have a progressive set of calls to action that ultimately lead to a sale by progressively increasing your engagement level with your consumer and slowly earning the right to ask for more information and close a sale.

Your call to action should flow naturally from your marketing goals and objectives. Below are some examples of calls to action based on different marketing strategies:

Marketing Goal	Call to Action
Lead Generation – >	Sign up for webinar
	Call for consultation
	Complete form for consultation

*Note that the lead generation
calls to action all result in gaining contact information.*

Build Awareness – >	Watch video
	Click on links
	Read content

Fan/Friend/Follow brand

Sign up for newsletter

Note that the awareness calls to
action simply aim to educate and engage consumers.

While your ultimate desired action is probably to drive or generate a sale, the best way to get there often involves intermediate steps that end in driving a sale.

Think of dating and meeting someone at a bar. While your ultimate objective in meeting someone may be marriage, or sexual activities, there are a number of intermediate steps that lead to the ultimate close. First you strike up a conversation, and see if you actually have anything in common (building initial awareness). Next you may ask for a telephone number (the first conversion). The next objective is to schedule a date (second conversion). At the end of the date, a goodnight kiss may make up the next conversion and so on. Opening with "I'm looking for marriage, what about you?" can seem aggressive and creepy. Instead, we create smaller conversions that lead us down the path to success. This is also how social media marketing objectives should be treated.

Getting to the sale is the final step in a chain of actions. For example, your chain to drive a sale may be -> Click on blog post from Twitter/ Facebook -> Sign up for email newsletter -> Sign up for webinar (collect lead scoring and contact information) -> Sales person call -> Purchase. In each instance, the goal is to increase the level of interaction and engagement and ultimately make a sale at the end. Creating small incremental steps can be very effective in ultimately getting someone to purchase.

Talking about Yourself Vs. Building an Army of Advocates

A final strategy point to consider when building your social media plan is to consider the value of building an "army" of passionate brand defenders, advocates and enthusiasts. Many businesses focus their social media efforts around talking about themselves, their business and publishing their own content. They measure social media based on the number of followers or mentions.

While social media is a valuable platform for businesses to share their content, it can be an even more powerful platform for building an "army" of people who are passionate about your business. These people will talk about you to their friends – *not* because of a contest you are running – because they are really, truly passionate about your business. They love you and want to tell the world.

Building and cultivating these relationships can deliver real business value. First, this is the basic "word-of-mouth marketing" that we previously discussed. Building relationships, and rewarding and giving attention to your fans are key drivers of word-of-mouth. In addition, these are the people who will come to your defense if you land yourself in hot water.

When I worked at a photography start-up we had a very passionate brand advocate. He actually started off as a brand enemy – he had posted a number of negative comments about our business after a misunderstanding in our FAQ. I immediately contacted him, had a quick phone conversation with him and explained the situation. He was flattered that I had taken the time to personally call him. He set up Google Alerts for our company, and left positive comments on every blog post that was written about our company. He also recommended us and defended us in discussion forums.

You can't buy that kind of natural positive recommendation. We never compensated him – we sent him some promotional items and gave him "sneak peaks" at new features. By cultivating a relationship with him, he became our biggest brand advocate, and we saw conversions come from discussion forums where he recommended us.

An additional value of brand advocates comes when you get into trouble. Sooner or later, most businesses do something that offends or upsets someone. Having honest, regular people, who are not compensated, defend you can turn an entire conversation around. Advocates can be one of your greatest social media assets.

We'll discuss an extension of the concept, working with influencers, in the Social Media PR chapter.

ACTION ITEMS AND KEY LEARNINGS

Want to put the Social Media Field Guide into Action?
Go to www.bootcampdigital.com/actionplanner to
download your FREE Field Guide action planner.

CHAPTER 3:

Target Audience – The Terrain

Once your marketing strategies have been defined, you know where you need to go. You have your destination clearly plotted out on the map. The next step is to understand your target audience. Who are you trying to reach with your message?

In continuing with the Social Marketing System, the next step in creating a social media plan is to understand your target audience and buyer personas. A deep understanding of your consumer – who they are, what they like, their behavior, their demographics, their psychographics – is key to the next stage of the Social Marketing System: your content.

49

Linking Your Target to Your Marketing Goals

When defining your target audience, the key to success is to link back to your marketing goals and objectives. Are you targeting new customers or existing customers? Is it related to a specific new product? Your marketing goals should provide you with an understanding of whom you are trying to reach. But in order to be successful in social media marketing and to develop a meaningful content plan, you have to be even more targeted and specific.

The key first step in defining your target audience is to link back to your marketing goals and objectives and really get as specific as possible. Are you looking to reach consumers who have already used a competitive product or who are new to the category? For example, if your objective is to reach new customers, are you looking to transition customers who are using a competitive product or are you looking to have customers choose you when they are initially entering the category?

Answering these questions as they pertain to your marketing goals will put you on the right path to selecting a target audience.

Getting Specific: The Bullseye

The most successful social media marketing plans are the ones that are the most targeted. Many businesses define their target audience very broadly: a tax accountant may say "anyone who pays taxes" or a food company may say "people who eat." These broadly defined audiences don't lend themselves very well to a specific marketing plan. With a little thought and effort, most target audiences can become much more defined. Businesses that cannot clearly and specifically define their target audience typically waste a lot of time and money in all of their marketing efforts. The more specifically you can define your ideal target audience, the more effectively you can create a marketing plan directed to them.

Think of a target with a bullseye in the center. The outer ring of the target represents all of the people who may be interested in your product, like "people who eat" or "people who pay taxes." These are all potential candidates for your product. The outer ring defines anyone who could possibly use your product.

If we move in one layer we have likely candidates for your product. These are people who are most likely to use your product. For example, if you have a food company that makes health products, the second ring of the bullseye may be "people who watch their weight." The tax accountant may say "businesses that need taxes completed." This ring is a little more specific. It is one step closer to a specific target audience. These are people who could likely use or buy your product or services. They represent your current client base (or if you are a new business, your ideal client base).

The bullseye is the most important part of the target. This is even more specific than the general group of people who use your product or service.

These are the people who you really designed your product for. They have a very specific problem that you are helping to solve. For example, if you are the diet food company, the bullseye may be "busy women on-the-go who are concerned about weight but don't have time to cook meals at home. They are typically professional women with families." This is MUCH more specific than "people who eat food." For the tax accountant it may be "small businesses that don't have an accounting firm on retainer. They typically maintain their own books but need help with taxes."

Getting as specific as possible in defining this audience will help you market your business more effectively. While there are a broad range of people who may potentially use your product or service, it is probably designed to solve a problem or pain point for a much more specific group of people. Just as you would aim for the bullseye of an archery target or dartboard, you should aim your marketing efforts at this clearly defined group.

As a side note, defining your target specifically doesn't mean that you will only accept clients who are within the specific target that you design for. For example, if you look at an ad for Tide laundry detergent, they are clearly targeting moms with 2 kids, a dog and a mini van. I buy Tide although I have no children, no pets and no mini van. Targeting isn't about limiting yourself, it is about focusing yourself.

Creating Personas

Creating personas of your buyers or customers is a great way to gain an even deeper understanding of your target audience. Social media marketing involves having conversational and intimate interactions with real people about things that they are interested in. Looking at your potential "buyers" or customers as complete people and painting an image of them will help you do this more effectively. Most businesses will have multiple personas as there are different use-cases for their product or service.

According to Wikipedia[24]:

> **Personas** are fictional characters created to represent the different user types within a targeted demographic, attitude and/or behavior set that might use a brand or

---

24 http://en.wikipedia.org/wiki/Persona_(marketing)

product in a similar way. Personas are a tool or method of market segmentation.

Personas are useful in considering the goals, desires, and limitations of brand buyers and users in order to help to guide decisions about a service, product or interaction space such as features, interactions, and visual design of a website.

A **user persona** is a representation of the goals and behavior of a real group of users. In most cases, personas are synthesized from data collected from interviews with users. They are captured in 1–2 page descriptions that include behavior patterns, goals, skills, attitudes, and environment, with a few fictional personal details to make the persona a realistic character. For each product, more than one persona is usually created, but one persona should always be the primary focus for the design.

Essentially, a buyer persona is a detailed profile of an example buyer that represents the real audience. Beyond demographic information, it includes their behavior, interests, goals, skills, attitudes, family and life situation, hobbies, etc. The goal is to create an actual person who represents your target audience. By thinking about the needs of a fictitious persona, marketers and designers are better able to infer the interests of a real person in a given situation.

Politicians in their political campaigns often use personas. Bill Clinton and George W. Bush both campaigned to "soccer moms" during the elections. The presidents' campaign staff uses dozens of personas like these to help focus their message and earn more votes[25]. In the 2008 election, Republican Vice Presidential Nominee Sarah Palin famously referred to "Joe Six-Pack and Hockey Moms" during a debate and the Presidential Candidate John McCain referenced Joe the Plumber when talking about how tax plans could hurt average Americans[26]. The political references are not intended to get into a discussion about political marketing, rather they

25 http://www.buyerpersona.com/2006/11/whats_a_buyer_p.html

26 http://en.wikipedia.org/wiki/John_Q._Public

are used to highlight the universal use of personas in examples that most people are familiar with.

For success in digital marketing, it is vital to have a deep understanding of your target consumer so you can develop compelling and relevant content. Each persona will have different interests, needs and personalities, and your content strategy should be targeted to the specific personas that will help you achieve your marketing objectives. Taking the time to create personas for your key stakeholders will help you develop a content plan that really resonates with your audience.

Where Is Your Audience Online?

Once you know who your audience *is* through creating buyer personas, the next step is to understand where they spend their time online. In social media marketing, you will want to build relationships and connections with your target group online, so understanding where they are online is vital to success.

Some of the questions to ask are:

- What news sites do they go to?
- What discussion forums do they participate in?
- Are there niche community sites?
- What social networks are they active on?
- What do they do on each social network and how active are they?
- What sharing sites are they active on?
- Do they have groups on these sites?
- Are there niche online groups that they are a part of?
- What blogs do they read?
- Who are the influential bloggers?
- Who is influential on Twitter?
- Who are the community leaders?
- Are they members of organizations?
- What social news sites are they a part of?

What Do They Talk about?

After understanding *where* they are online, gain an understanding of *what* they talk about. What are the subject areas they are passionate about and interested in? What areas do they have questions about? Look at other blogs or news sites in your industry – what stories or articles get the most comments or are the most popular? Understanding what they want to talk about is the next important step to understand your target audience.

When I worked at the photography website startup we spent a lot of time online trying to understand what our target audience was interested in. We developed 2 key insights. The first was that they were very passionate about photographers' rights. Blog posts about a camera being confiscated or a photographer being told not to take photos by police generated hundreds of comments, and photographers showed genuine passion and concern for this. We used this as a core content area for our corporate blog and were able to generate over 20 posts by writing on photographers' rights issues. It also built positive equity with photographers since "we were on their side" and shared a passion with them. Photographers felt that we really understood them, even though we did not have an actual photographer on our staff.

The second key insight that we used as a basis for our content was that photographers had a lot of questions about the legal issues pertaining to photography. We saw *many* discussion forum posts about model releases and legal rights when using photos and there weren't any great resources. We used this knowledge to hire a lawyer to write a weekly column on our content driven blog. The legal column generated a TON of interest and comments because we produced content that met genuine information need.

By listening to conversations and really understanding what your audience likes to talk about, what they need to know and what topics capture their enthusiasm, you will be able to develop a powerful and meaningful content plan.

How Do They Talk?

Once you understand who your target audience is, where they spend their time online and what they are interested in talking about, the next key area to understand is *how* they talk to each other.

This was discussed in Chapter 2 under "Listen and Observe." When you get involved in social media marketing, you will aim to develop real relationships with your target audience. This means being able to relate to them, use their words and sound like one of them. Depending on your brand positioning and equity you may or may not choose to sound like your target audience; however, it is important to understand how they talk to each other and the words that they use to describe things.

Building common ground with your audience by sounding like one of them will help you gain acceptance not just in social media, but in the rest of your marketing as well.

ACTION ITEMS AND KEY LEARNINGS

Want to put the Social Media Field Guide into Action?
Go to www.bootcampdigital.com/actionplanner to
download your FREE Field Guide action planner.

CHAPTER 4:

Rules of Engagement for Social Media – The Legend

The social media map is nearly complete. You know your destination (marketing goals) and your target audience (the terrain). The next step is to understand the legend. The legend helps you make sense of the entire map and defines the "rules" or "norms" for reading or navigating with the map. The legend in social media marketing is the rules of engagement. What are the rules or norms of social media interactions?

Many marketers and individuals find social media difficult to navigate – there are many unwritten practices and rules of etiquette that social media participants are expected to abide by. Slip up and you could encounter the wrath of bloggers or be labeled a spammer.

This chapter will provide you with principles for success in social media, as well as rules of engagement and how to avoid being "that guy." Something to keep in mind when engaging in social media is that you are participating in *social* discussions taking place by *real people* about *real things* that they care about. You are attempting to *earn* their attention on their turf, which means you need to play by their rules.

Treat people's social media – their blog, Twitter stream, Facebook page, etc. – as though you were entering their house. Depending on the circumstances, you may have been invited (they requested to follow you) or you may be dropping in unannounced (you are following them and hoping to *earn* their attention or interest). Take your shoes off at the door and wait to be invited in. Build some rapport. Don't barge in demanding a cold beer and a hot meal. Wait to be offered. Or make a polite request after settling in to a discussion. Your first interaction should never be a request for something – especially when dropping by without an invitation!

Permission Vs. Interruption Marketing

Seth Godin coined the concept of permission marketing versus interruption marketing. Old media or traditional marketing relies heavily on interruption marketing. Brands pay money to earn the right to interrupt you and demand your attention. TV advertising, magazine ads, billboards, pop-up ads, and radio ads – all are created to interrupt you from what you are doing (trying to watch a show, listen to the radio, etc.), and instead advertise at you. Marketers in interruption marketing don't have to worry about whether or not you *want* to see their ad – they paid for the right to make you watch it. And you understand that it is part of the "cost" you pay to consume the content (the TV show, radio, magazine, etc.).

The content of interruption ads is focused around how to best sell the product. It doesn't matter if the viewer has any interest in the ad or finds it useful. The goal of the ad is to showcase the product and benefits to sell the product. Many of the most boring ads are actually very effective at selling products.

The key to successful interruption content is to position and sell the product. Attention does not have to be earned, it is bought.

Permission-based marketing, on the other hand, is earned. Permission marketing is when consumers give you permission to market to them. Your marketing adds value and consumers welcome and request to receive your marketing messages. Opting in to your email newsletter, following you on Twitter, signing up for text message alerts, etc., are all examples of permission marketing. Social media is about permission marketing. Consumers choose to follow/friend/read/listen/watch because of the inherent value of your marketing.

The problem is that people are bombarded by ads. According to the Media Dynamics publication, Media Matters, a typical adult is exposed to 600 – 625 ads per day[27]. Ads have been seen on urinal cakes, the backs of restroom stalls, napkins, airline peanuts and even on sheep! Consumers are becoming increasingly blind to much of this advertising. We fast-forward commercials and change the station when an ad comes on the radio. There is also a growing trend towards "banner blindness" that shows that consumers know where to expect ads on a web page and that their eyes don't even focus on the ads. They are able to completely block out the ads because their peripheral vision can see them and ignore them.

How can you possibly build your brand and gain attention in the sea of advertising? Unless you have millions of dollars to spend, you probably can't. The answer is social media and permission-based marketing.

In a permission-based marketing model, the size of your budget matters less and the size of your passion and personality matters more. Permission marketing evens the playing field.

The catch? You can't buy your way in. You have to *earn* it. That is what makes social media marketing difficult to navigate – it requires that you *earn* attention from people who *have a choice* about whether or not they engage with you. People are choosing to engage with brands that are authentic, transparent, that care, show empathy, respect them, respect their time, respect their opinions and are human.

The good news is that if you do it well, the ROI (return on investment) can be huge. Brands and businesses are witnessing tremendous growth by observing the rules of permission-based marketing.

Social media requires permission-based or earned marketing. Marketers don't have the *right* to be on my Twitter stream, in my Facebook page or on my blog. They have to *earn* the right and have my permission (implicit or explicit) to market at me. If they annoy me or accost me with

---

27 http://ams.aaaa.org/eweb/upload/FAQs/adexposures.pdf

uninvited sales pitches I will cut them off (at best) or possibly go so far as to flame them on my blog or in my Twitter stream.

When approaching social media marketing, it is important to ease your way in. Start small. Listen first and slowly begin participating once you understand your community, their language, the etiquette and the conversation (as discussed in Chapter 2).

Principles for Success

To be successful in a permission-based social media marketing world, it is essential that you provide the community (your audience) with something of value. In his book, Marketing with Meaning[1], Bob Gilbreath talks about the importance of creating marketing that itself adds value as a way of earning the attention of your target audience. People spend time online for three basic reasons: to connect with people, to get information or to be entertained. Your social media strategy has to appeal to one of these three reasons.

Successful social media strategies typically meet one (or more) of the **PARC** principles for success by being participatory, authentic, relevant and credible.

Participatory

Brands that are successful on social media are participatory. They interact with the community, answer questions and say thank you. They participate in the community and the existing groups and events. They gain exposure with new audiences by being "one of them" and participating where they are. Big brands have a tendency to want to run their own show and create their own community, groups and events. If there is a genuine need, by all means, create your own. In most cases there are existing communities – earn trust by showing and interest and participating. Play on the terms of the community and support their events.

Be ready to respond, and be conversational. In social media there is an expectation of two-way communication. There is an expectation that businesses will respond to blog comments, tweets or Facebook posts. Be ready and open to conversations and participate in the community.

Authentic

Authenticity is vital to the success of any social media marketing campaign. With the Internet, a proliferation of information is spreading faster than you can imagine.

There is more information spreading quicker than ever before, so strategies that are deceptive or lack authenticity run the risk of being outed. In the age of information, a lack of authenticity is a sure fire way to lose credibility and respect for you and your brand.

But authenticity is more than just not lying. Authenticity means talking to real people like an authentic real person. Be personable. Share some personal information. People connect with real people who they feel a connection with. Putting a human face to the brand helps build connections with real people. Providing an honest and sincere response can earn goodwill, trust and ultimately business.

By being authentic, businesses can build a positive brand reputation and put a human face to the business.

Consider this cease and desist letter from Jack Daniel's. As you can see, being personable and authentic, even when issuing legal letters, can earn goodwill – people just want to be treated well.

We are certainly flattered by your affection for the brand, but while we can appreciate the pop culture appeal of Jack Daniel's, we also have to be diligent to ensure that the Jack Daniel's trademarks are used correctly. Given the brand's popularity, it will probably come as no surprise that we come across designs like this on a regular basis. What may not be so apparent, however, is that if we allow uses like this one, we run the very real risk that our trademark will be weakened. As a fan of the brand, I'm sure that is not something you intended or would want to see happen.

As an author, you can certainly understand our position and the need to contact you. You may even have run into similar problems with your own intellectual property.

In order to resolve this matter, because you are both a Louisville "neighbor" and a fan of the brand, we simply request that you change the cover design when the book is re-printed. If you would be willing to change the design sooner than that (including on the digital version), we would be willing to contribute a reasonable amount towards the costs of doing so. By taking this step, you will help us to ensure that the Jack Daniel's brand will mean as much to future generations as it does today.

Relevant

In permission marketing, businesses have to be useful and relevant. One of the best ways to do this is to be resourceful – provide your audience with helpful information. Providing your audience with a genuinely useful resource is a great way to earn trust and attention in social media.

There are many potential ways that your brand can be a resource online. You can use social media to solve customer service problems or deal with complaints. If you tweet the airline @jetblue[2], a customer service rep will answer your question or help solve your problem remarkably quickly.

Many B-to-B companies like HubSpot are relevant by sharing expert information with their audience. For example, HubSpot, which provides Internet marketing software, is relevant with a blog loaded with online marketing tips, and they also run webinars and provide free eBooks. Being relevant is about providing information that is useful, entertaining or helpful to your audience.

Being a resource to others positions your business as the experts that understand and care about the needs of your target audience. Sharing simple how-to videos or articles or compiling lists of recommended resources are great social media strategies.

Credible

Social media can be a powerful way for your organization to earn the trust of your audience by being credible. This is often referred to as demonstrating "*thought leadership*" – showcasing your original thoughts and ideas related to your products or your industry in general. This is especially useful in BtoB markets or for those trying to build a personal brand.

There are two sides to credibility. The first is building your credibility as a knowledgeable and expert organization, and the second is building credibility as a trusted organization.

To build the second type of credibility, businesses have to be ready to share information and be open to explaining rationale to their constituents. Businesses gain credibility by admitting their problems, asking the community for understanding or support and taking action to fix things. By communicating openly, businesses can build credibility.

Rules of Engagement

Social media involves *earning permission* to join in *personal conversations* with *real people* who don't want to be advertised at. They want you to add value to their lives. Being aware of the following rules of engagement will help you avoid common mistakes businesses make when entering social media.

1. Use Social Media Channels as Intended

Use all social media channels and their different communication methods as intended. Be aware of how the community is using channels and stick within the existing norms of communication. When using a social media channel look at the intended use as well as how the community is using it, and keep your use within these standards.

Take time to observe before jumping in. I participate in a number of groups on LinkedIn, each of which has different norms and rules of engagement. On some groups promoting yourself can get you kicked off. Others are nothing but self-promoters. In order to be effective, protect your brand and not offend others, it is important to understand and observe group norms.

For example, on Twitter users have the opportunity to send a tweet, which is a general public message to all followers, or a direct message, which is a direct message that is specifically sent to an individual. Some people unfamiliar with this channel send direct messages promoting their blog/business/product to all of their Twitter followers. An untargeted message for all followers should be sent as a tweet, not a direct message. Failing to follow site-specific conventions is one of the quickest ways to get unfollowed or called out on social media sites and is a mistake made by people new to Twitter and "social media experts" alike.

2. Don't Be a Dirty Spammer

Don't send people in your network unwanted messages without their permission. Just because they follow you does not mean that they want you to send them self-promotional or sales messages.

One of my LinkedIn connections downloaded his entire list of LinkedIn contacts and sent an email promoting some of his new products. This, in my opinion, is a form of spam. By connecting with him as an individual on LinkedIn, I was not opting-in or giving him permission to include me on mass emails. Second, he violated rule #1 by using a channel (LinkedIn) outside of how it is intended. If I requested to be included or opted-in to his email list, I would expect emails. Taking my email from LinkedIn to email me is a violation of my trust.

Give your audience the option to opt-out (or better yet, only message those who have opted in) and don't mass message people without their permission.

Sending unsolicited mass messages is a quick way to lose trust and annoy people.

3. *Assume People Don't Care About Your Product*

Related to the last rule on spamming, it is helpful to assume that most people on social media sites don't really care about your product. Sure, some might. But most people don't. They care about saving money or solving a problem.

Even those who follow your business on social networks are looking for something that is valuable to them, and an endless stream of press releases usually isn't very interesting.

Ask yourself – what is in it for them? Why would they care? WHO would actually want to read this message?

Many social media sites fail to gain traction because they have no clear audience and their content is only about their business. If you consistently provide real value to your audience you earn the right to talk about your business periodically. For example, a business I follow shares great tips for entrepreneurs. Since I love their tips, I have grown to respect and admire their company. Every now and again (maybe one in every 5 posts) they share something promotional, and I enjoy learning about their new products or features.

Endless self-promotion will probably only lead to people tuning out and ignoring you.

4. *Have a Personality*

Some people are hesitant to be personal on public social media sites. They want to keep their content strictly professional and business related.

The reality is that people connect with other human people on a deeper level than they connect with brands.

Sharing some of your personality helps build common ground and trust. If I feel like I know you and we have things in common, I am more likely to want to do business with you.

You don't want to get too personal and share your most intimate details, but sharing bands that you like or your addiction to coffee – harmless character traits – builds common ground and connections. Try to inject some personality into your social media efforts and don't take yourself too seriously.

5. *Provide Context to Connections*

Many social networks are intended for you to connect with people you already know. Facebook and LinkedIn are both sites where your network should be built around people that you actually already know.

When sending a request to connect with someone - whether it is on Twitter, Facebook, LinkedIn or even email - it is helpful to provide context to the connection. Why are you connecting with the person and how do you know each other?

Providing context is simple and just requires a quick note: "Hi John – I saw that we are both members of group X and you have posted some really smart discussion topics. I would like to add you to my network", or "Hi Sally. We met last week at a networking event and I wanted to follow up and say hi. You mentioned you were interested in social media marketing, so I went ahead and added you to my newsletter distribution. If you are not interested I'd be happy to take you off the list."

Adding a simple note of context will lead to higher acceptance rates on connection requests.

6. *Be Transparent*

Social media has changed the way information flows. Information is now available quickly and it travels across the world in an instant. This means that businesses have to be more transparent in their interactions.

Consumers can talk to each other. They can read about each other's experiences. They can research your company. They can research you.

This means that companies have to be upfront and honest. Consumer reviews will highlight issues or problems. Be prepared to address them in an open and honest manner. The walls are falling – be prepared for what is on the other side.

7. *Talk about the Topic*

Businesses will often find discussion threads, Twitter conversations, groups or blog posts that are related to their business line. Often times their first instinct is to jump in to the conversation with a marketing message. Don't.

By all means, join the conversation, but talk about what the conversation is about, not what you want it to be about. You know that guy at the cocktail parties who loudly brags about himself the whole time? No matter what you say to change the topic he always manages to bring it back to himself? Don't be that guy.

A company I trained sold down comforters. When they began participating in discussion forums they searched for conversations about comforters and would often provide a discount on their products. For example, on a discussion thread about *How to Remove Coffee Stains from a Down Comforter* they would respond with *Why not just buy a new one? We'll even give you 25% off with this coupon code.* This wasn't very effective. They were often removed from conversations and received negative feedback. Plus, they weren't generating a lot of sales.

Over time they evolved their strategy and created a blog with lots of relevant and useful information. Now when they see a conversation about how to clean a down comforter, they refer to a video blog post that shows directions. They found that by staying on topic and providing useful information they gained trust and ultimately sold more products.

Talk about the conversation topic that is being addressed, not about your product or service. Don't hijack the conversation and try to shift it for your own best interest. People see through this and you can lose trust or even be kicked out of the group or off of the site.

8. *My Social Media Profile Is Not Your Billboard*

Keep in mind that social media profiles are NOT created for you to market on. When I started working in social media I worked at a photography start up and I learned this the hard way. We thought we had a great product and that photographers would really love it. We searched for blog posts that talked about our topic area and left messages letting them know about our site. We thought we were doing them a favor. Little did we know…

Within minutes we got nasty responses back from bloggers asking us not to post our marketing material on their site. In our minds we were being helpful. In their minds we were being inappropriate.

Don't use other people's social media profiles or websites as a way to promote your message. Stick to the conversations that are actually already taking place.

9. *Be Nice*

Sounds simple, right? It is. Yet many businesses have a hard time grasping this. Just remember what your mother told you – always say please and thank you.

A simple thank you can go a long way. Look for opportunities to publicly or privately thank people who help you out or say nice things about you. If you are asking for something, ask nicely and don't ask for too much.

Many years ago a good friend of mine, Saul Colt, was running marketing for an online invoicing company. They wanted to be the nicest company on the Internet. When one of their Twitter followers posted that she had been stood up on a date they sent her flowers. Seriously, they had flowers delivered to her just to be nice. They earned tons of goodwill and the story spread through the web.

Look for opportunities to give back to other people in your community. Promote their events or blog posts or products. Share the wealth. In the long run you'll get back more than what you give.

Start with a Passive Strategy

When engaging in social media, there are two types of engagement: passive and active. For big brands that may have risks to participation or businesses that are still getting their feet wet, it can be helpful to begin with a passive strategy and evolve into a more active strategy. Get your feet wet, test the water and then jump in.

A Passive Strategy – Search, Listen and Respond

If you are new to social media, starting with a more passive approach is a good way to get started. This links back to the first step of the social media marketing cycle – listening.

In this passive approach to social media, start by searching out mentions of your business, your competitors or your category or industry. Spend time listening to what people are saying. Once you are comfortable with the conversations, you can begin by responding. In Chapter 13 on Public Relations we cover responding to social media in detail.

Responses can be relatively simple – "Thanks for including our product in your blog post. We really appreciate it. Please give me a call if you have any feedback or additional comments." Simply saying thank you and answering questions is a great first step.

Get a feel for the landscape, the hot issues and the opportunities. In a case study on Pinterest that I researched for my book *Visual Social Media Marketing,* a national brand spent months researching, understanding and preparing before launching a very successful Pinterest campaign. Don't be afraid to spend time learning upfront – this will increase your chances of success.

ACTION ITEMS AND KEY LEARNINGS

Want to put the Social Media Field Guide into Action?
Go to www.bootcampdigital.com/actionplanner to
download your FREE Field Guide action planner.

PART 2:

The Social Media Field Guide

At this point we've covered the foundations of your social media marketing plan – the map or plan to success. After listening, clearly defining marketing strategies and identifying the target audience, the next steps are to develop content, select tools, implement, measure and adjust.

The content, tools and implementation are covered in Part 2 of the book, "The Field Guide." The field guide section is focused on building and executing a social media marketing plan that leverages best practices.

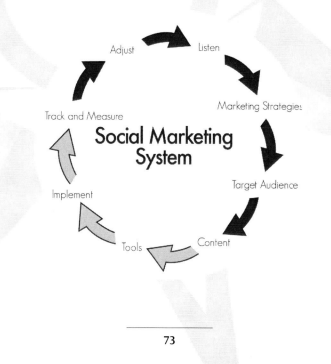

CHAPTER 5:

Introduction to the Field Guide

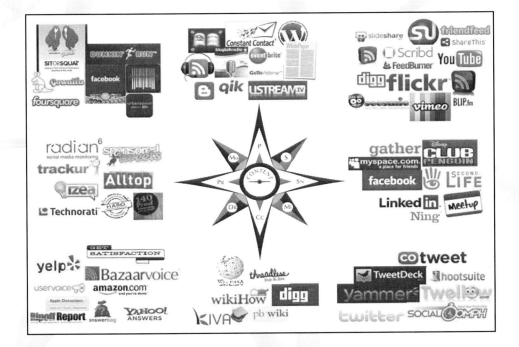

Companies face two primary problems when they initially approach social media.

The first problem that companies and organizations often face is how to strategically approach social media. The best results in social media (and any type of marketing for that matter) are achieved when you start with your objectives (to get new customers, increase loyalty, etc.), understand your target audience and have compelling content (in advertising the content is "the big idea" or creative). This challenge was addressed in the first section of the book.

The second challenge is how to make sense of the social media landscape and choose the right tools. With thousands of social media websites and tools, it can be difficult to understand the landscape and to prioritize social media marketing opportunities. This is something that I have seen with my training and consulting clients again and again. A CEO in my executive coaching program recently said, "There are just too many options, and it seems like they change every day. How are we supposed to stay on top of this? How do we know which ones are worth investing our time and energy in?" This is a legitimate concern. The problem is that he is looking at a mish-mash of different websites versus thinking about social media in a strategic and organized way.

Many brands approach social media with the end in mind – "I want a Facebook page or a Twitter account" – without thinking it through strategically. There is more to social media than just having a profile or account –you need to know how to effectively implement it into your business plan. That is where the Social Media Field Guide comes in.

In the world of social media, brands have to earn the right for your attention. This means businesses need a great content plan; a brand has to create something that is so interesting/useful/entertaining that people will want to engage in your marketing and your brand message.

The Social Media Field Guide Explained

The Social Media Field Guide provides a framework for understanding the social media landscape and helps navigate it to make sound social media marketing decisions.

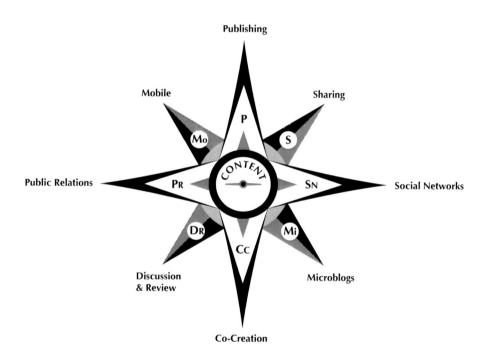

The Social Media Field Guide will help brands strategically approach social media by making sense of the key strategic choices and the social media landscape that drives this decision-making.

At the core of the Field Guide is content. Content is absolutely vital to the success of any social media plan, which is why it is in the center of the Field Guide. As discussed earlier, as the market has shifted from interruption advertising to permission social media marketing, consumers now have the right to opt-out of marketing. To keep them engaged, marketing has to be interesting/useful/entertaining. The marketing or content itself has to add value.

Once you understand the content, the next step is to decide which direction to go in. Social media offers a wide variety of tools, websites and applications that brands and individuals can use. It can be difficult to make sense of all of the options and think strategically. The Social Media Field Guide is designed around 8 directions or types of social media websites. The 8 directions in the Social Media Field Guide are publishing, sharing, social networks, micro-blogs, collaboration and co-creation, discussion and review, public relations and mobile. Every social media website, application, tool or widget falls into one of these 8 directions.

While the specific tools of social media may change, the directions remain relatively constant. For example, Friendster was the first popular social network, followed by MySpace, and today we have Facebook and LinkedIn. If you were reading this book 5 years ago, MySpace would have been one of the big focus areas. Today, only a few niche businesses are interested in MySpace, like music and low-income marketers.

While the websites or tools have changed considerably over time, the concept of social networking or connecting with other people online hasn't changed. In this respect, the directions of the Social Media Field Guide are constant. By focusing your social media strategies on the direction first and the tool second, your marketing plan will be able to sustain over long time periods because it won't be reliant on an individual tool.

Additionally, selecting the social media marketing direction before the tool leads to more strategic tool choices. For example, many businesses start by saying that they want a Facebook fan page; however, for their content and marketing objectives, perhaps a video series would be more appropriate and Facebook could be used as a syndication channel.

The 8 Directions of the Social Media Field Guide

Once you have determined the appropriate content, the next step is to determine which types of social media tools will generate the most success based on your marketing strategy. This is when you will choose the directions from the Social Media Field Guide. There are 8 directions in the Social Media Field Guide, and a chapter is dedicated to each one in this book.

The 8 directions represent the general categories that comprise the social media landscape by grouping social media technologies and sites into different buckets – Publishing, Sharing, Social Networks, Micro-Blogging, Co-Creation & Collaboration, Discussion & Review, PR and Mobile. There are overlaps between the tools in each. For example, Digg.com is a social news site where users can submit news stories and vote for what makes the front page. In this way, Digg is both a sharing site (you can submit or share news articles) and also a co-creation site (social voting determines the front page news). Arguments could also be made that microblogging should not be a separate circle – that it is naturally a social network, or a publishing site or a sharing site. Due to its size and uniqueness versus other social sites, we chose to create a separate direction for it.

When selecting a direction from the Social Media Field Guide, remember that the directions are not mutually exclusive. In fact, social media marketing works best when multiple social media channels are used together in an integrated fashion. For example, a publishing strategy requires syndication channels, like sharing, social networks and Twitter.

Below is an overview of the different directions of the social media landscape:

- **Publishing** – Publishing is creating your own content to post online. This includes blogs, email newsletters, podcasts, webinars, white papers and e-books – where specific valuable content is created and syndicated online.

- **Sharing** – Sharing is when you share content like photos and videos through social sites on the web. Sharing can also include news and webpages – anything that spreads through the web. This section includes both sharing your own content and encouraging others to share.

- **Social networks** – Social networks like Facebook and LinkedIn allow people to build relationships and connections on the web. In addition to large social networks, there are also niche and customized social networks.

- **Microblogging** – The main microblogging is Twitter, a social network where people share short 140 character updates with their "followers." There are also many tools and applications to help manage Twitter accounts.

- **Co-creation and collaboration** – Social media has allowed for more opportunities for people to work together and create content in an easy and seamless way. Wikis, like Wikipedia.com, allow many people to edit and create content.

- **Discussion and review** – Discussion and review sites have been around much longer than the term "social media." Essentially, these sites allow people to share their opinions on products or other subjects. Sites like Amazon.com have incorporated discussion and review right into their website.

- **Public relations** – PR in the advent of social media requires a different approach than before. Since everyone has a voice, public relations now includes the public (versus just the press) and there is more emphasis on leveraging bloggers and online influencers versus just traditional press.

- **Mobile** – Social media is increasingly going mobile with geo-location social networks like Foursquare and Gowalla that share your location with your friends. In addition to these sites, regular social networks have mobile applications and there are many new branded social networks that serve specific purposes, like Dunkin Run.

The 8 directions represent the core categories that social media sites and technologies represent. In speaking to thousands of people about social media marketing, there is a fixation on the tools – I want Facebook, I want LinkedIn. However, a more strategic approach focuses first on the circles – I want to create content, I want to share content – and then on the particular tools.

Choosing Your Direction

Selecting from the 8 directions is the next step in building your social media content plan. Different circles are more appropriate for different budgets, resources and content. We will discuss each direction in detail in the upcoming chapters. Once you have selected the most appropriate directions for your social media marketing strategy, you can select the best tools.

Selecting Your Sites

After choosing the direction that makes the most sense for your marketing strategy, target audience and content, you'll have to select the tool. For example, if you select social networks as a key way to deliver your content, you can then choose between Facebook, LinkedIn, MySpace, niche sites or creating your own social network. The key to selecting the right tool is to ask a few strategic questions.

1) Is the target audience there?

2) Do I have the right content for the site?

3) How does the site let me market?

4) How do I need to adapt my content for this medium?

5) Does my audience want to connect here?

1. Is the target audience there?

Are you fishing where the fish are? Is your target audience active and engaged in this tool? For example, LinkedIn has an older and more professional audience versus Facebook. The average LinkedIn user is 44 years old whereas the average Facebook user is 38 years old[28]. Sure there are millions of people on Twitter, but is your target audience there? The first step in selecting the tool is to determine if your target audience is on that particular site.

2. Do you have the right content?

The next question to ask yourself is whether or not you have the right type of content for the site that you are interested in. For example, you may find that your audience is active on YouTube, but you may not have video content that you can create to grab attention. 70% of bloggers are organically talking about brands on their blogs29. If you can capture your audience, you will give them something to talk about.

---

28 http://royal.pingdom.com/2010/01/16/study-ages-of-social-network-users/

29 http://econsultancy.com/
       blog/5324-20+-mind-blowing-social-media-statistics-revisited#comments

Different types of content also work well in different social sites depending on the audience you want to reach. If you are trying to explain something complex, YouTube might work better than audio podcasting. If you have a really dynamic figurehead on your company, you may want to leverage video sharing sites. Select the sites that best match your content.

3. Does the site allow you to market effectively?

Social sites have different terms of service or rules for how businesses can participate. Many of these rules specifically discuss what companies can and cannot do to market their products or businesses on the sites. A site might be great for your content and might also have your target audience, but if they have strict policies about marketing or corporate participation, they may not work for you.

For example, you may find that your audience is on LinkedIn and that they are really receptive to videos. LinkedIn does not allow you to share videos (although you could post links to blog posts) but Facebook does. Therefore, Facebook would be a better site for you because it is more flexible in how marketers can use the site.

A quick note about terms of service of social networking sites (and all sites for that matter) - pay attention to the terms of service and don't violate them. Violation can result in the removal of your account and possibly legal action. I know a number of individuals and companies that have been banned from sites like Facebook and LinkedIn and had their accounts removed. If you invest a lot of time and effort into building up your presence on a social website, you do not want to have it taken down for a terms of service violation.

4. How do you adapt your content for the medium?

This is probably one of the biggest keys to success in social media marketing, as it is for any form of marketing. In traditional marketing, if you create a television ad you do not simply take the text from the TV commercial and a photo of it and throw it on a print magazine or a billboard. The same is true for social media. Content needs to be adapted for each medium to be successful.

Spending time in the listening stage across channels will help you understand how content should be structured to maximize results. An article that works well in a print magazine might fail as a blog post because consumers read differently online – they scan the text and like headlines and highly organized content.

Copywriting and creativity are the keys to success – you have to use the right words and build compelling concepts. On Twitter, you only have 140 characters to get a message across. Writing a killer tweet that is retweeted and read by others requires understanding of how to write for Twitter. A blog headline might work well for a blog, but a different headline for the same content could grab more attention on Twitter.

The same is true for video content. A great blog post read exactly into a video might not be very effective. However, the same content could be adjusted into a very compelling video by shortening it and adding personality, visuals and quick points.

The key is to understand the medium and test it to see how you need to adjust your content to be successful.

5. Does my audience WANT to connect there?

The last question to ask is where your audience is most receptive to your message. Your target group might be on Facebook and love videos, but if your video is about a work related topic, or something that they do not want to publicly share, they may not want to connect there. Knowing where your audience is receptive is vital to success. Typically, reaching them in a forum where they are already talking about your product is the most natural fit. For example, business topics on LinkedIn and general interests and social topics on Facebook might be a more appropriate location.

One word of caution: Do not assume that consumers will not want to talk business on social sites. I recently spoke to a group of CEOs as a part of my CEO and Executive coaching program and one of the CEOs mentioned, "Facebook is great for kids sharing photos, but my buyers are very technical. They don't want to talk about this stuff on Facebook. They probably aren't even on Facebook!" So, I did a quick Facebook search for his company and sure enough, they actually had a fan page that was created by an office in another country. We pulled up the fan page and a number of his clients were asking questions about his product on Facebook. "I know that guy!" he said about one of the questions, "Why would he ask that question here instead of calling us?!" Be where your customers are, be accessible and be open.

Regardless of what industry you are in, **you should interact with your customers and potential customers when, where and how they want to interact with you.** Write that down. Tell this to your boss or other stakeholders you have to convince to use social media. For all the dollars you spend on sales reps and customer service, you can lose the sale or the customer if you leave these questions unanswered.

What Marketers Are Using

Marketers are already using a variety of online tools to market their business and are leaning away from traditional services. According to a 2012 study from 62 Marketing, 41% of companies stated they are reducing investment on print media. 64% are stating they will place more investment into social media efforts, and 64% also say they're planning to increase their SEO budget. 70% of companies say they're intending to increase investment on social media networks like Facebook. (can you include a footnote to http://www.imediaconnection.com/content/32706.asp)

Additionally, businesses are using a wide variety of tools to connect with customers. According to a social media study Facebook, Twitter, LinkedIn, Blogs and Video are used by most marketers. Newer social networks like Pinterest and Instagram are not yet large enough to stand out on these surveys, yet these sites are seeing rapid adoption by consumers and marketers.

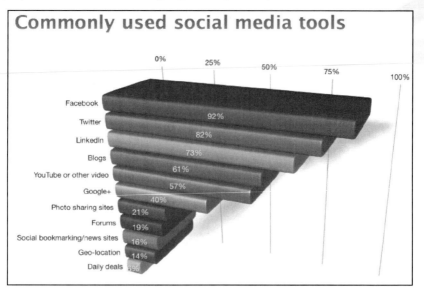

Commonly used social media tools

Facebook	92%
Twitter	82%
LinkedIn	73%
Blogs	61%
YouTube or other video	57%
Google+	40%
Photo sharing sites	21%
Forums	19%
Social bookmarking/news sites	16%
Geo-location	14%
Daily deals	

ACTION ITEMS AND KEY LEARNINGS

Want to put the Social Media Field Guide into Action?
Go to www.**bootcampdigital.com/actionplanner** to
download your FREE Field Guide action planner.

PART 2:

The Social Media Field Guide

CHAPTER 6:

Content

- - - - - - -

Content is the cornerstone and foundation of any social media marketing strategy and it is at the center of the Social Media Field Guide. Content marketing is emerging as a leading way for consumers to connect with brands online.

In social media, content is what you post – the status updates, images, videos, photos, words, etc.

The 2 Biggest Content Mistakes

Many companies make the mistake of not focusing on content or creating content that is brand-centric and not really interesting to the target audience. Companies that don't spend time thinking about their content are destined to fail on social media. Creating a fan page, blog, Twitter account or podcast that nobody listens to has no value. Even if you have lots of fans, likes or followers, if you don't consistently create great content, they won't even notice you. When you create any social media asset, the key first question is what content will really engage your audience?

For example, a small business owner that I met hired a "social media consultant" who created a Facebook fan page for the business. I asked whom they were trying to reach and they said, "new customers." Right away, an alarm bell went off for me since fan pages are typically best for connecting with existing customers versus finding new customers. The second question I asked was what their content plan was for the fan page. They didn't have an answer. They hadn't really thought about what the content should be. The "social media consultant" that they hired just set up the page and didn't spend any time working with the business on what the actual content should be. Sure, the business now had a fan page, but they didn't have a content plan that would actually interest their target audience, drive interactions and build marketing value.

The second big content mistake that businesses make on social media is posting brand-centric content. This is a very common mistake – brands want to use social media as a PR machine where they talk about their "awesome" initiatives and work that they are doing. As a listener, what is in it for me? Why do I want to hear about your achievements as a company? Sure, every now and again it is good to know what is going on, but a consistent PR machine isn't really interesting to me.

I was recently giving a keynote presentation, and spoke to an audience member who ran an auto repair shop. They recently joined social media and had just developed their content plan. They were planning to post photos and commentary about the cars that they were fixing. This is a flawed strategy for 2 reasons. First, it is an auto repair shop. Unless the repairs are unbelievable, everyone probably already knows that they repair cars. Posting about repaired cars is probably not serving a real marketing objective. Second, it is brand-centric public relations content. As a fan, follower or customer, what is in it for me? What do I get out of learning about all of the cars that they are repairing?

Instead, I recommended that they provide something useful to the target audience. Do a tutorial video on how to change your own oil (and I'm sure that it will look like WAY too much effort for anyone to want to do it themselves versus paying $20). Provide tips on car maintenance. Talk about what car care problems result in most of the repairs. Offer discounts or incentives.

Create a content plan that clearly has something in it for the audience. Don't focus on yourself.

Creating Great Content
Know Your Target – Know, Like and Trust

A deep understanding of your target audience is absolutely vital in creating relevant content. Not only do you have to know who your target audience is in terms of your marketing objectives (i.e., new customers, current customers, etc.), you have to know who your customers are as people. This can be achieved by creating Buyer Personas (covered in Chapter 3: The Social Media Map – Target Audience). This helps you grasp the real true interests of your target audience. In what areas related to your brand or product does your target audience take interest?

By learning about how your target audience interacts online you'll be able to interact in a way that gets their attention by being relevant (know), building common ground (like) and being authentic and genuine (trust).

Know

This deep understanding of the people you want to connect with will drive your content strategy. As mentioned previously, content is at the core of your social media strategic decision making. The content that drives your social media marketing strategy should be centered on something related to your brand that your target audience is really interested in and passionate about.

The key to discovering this is to spend some time online connecting with and interacting with your target audience. What content areas are they naturally talking about? What interests them? What do they forward, share on Facebook, tweet and re-tweet?

Like

In addition to just understanding what your audience talks about, it is important to understand how they talk. What tone do they interact in? Are they casual? Formal? Using swear words? Grammatically incorrect? Funny? Laid back? Understanding their natural tone and sentiment is important to being able to connect and build relationships. While taking on their tone may or may not match your brand, it is important to know how they talk so you can fit in.

When marketing in social media it is important to be relatable. Knowing what your audience can relate to and posting about shared experiences helps build the "like" factor. Show that you relate to them and understand them. Be nice. Offer support. Share your experiences. Create common ground.

Trust

Finally, build trust with your audience by being honest, open, authentic and transparent. Brands that are not authentic or who try to mislead people lose out online. In the age of user reviews and blogging, consumers have access to more information than ever. Be prepared to address issues head on and provide honest and reasonable responses to complaints.

Building trust online is about acting like a human and putting a human face to a company. A client that I worked with had an issue with a discussion forum where people were trashing one of his stores. It started with one post and quickly escalated as others sympathized or chimed in with their experiences. I coached the CEO to respond in a very personable way. He said he was really sorry to hear about the bad experience and that he would personally look in to it. He shared why they sometimes have these problems and his disappointment about the poor experience. The sentiment on the forum changed instantly. By taking ownership of the problem and relating to the complaint, he built trust and common ground. The comments completely changed – complainers now said that in fact, they primarily had very good experiences and they perhaps overreacted.

Work to build trust on social sites by taking ownership where appropriate and clearly explaining your positioning or point of view on controversial topics. Be as personable as possible – it is much harder to hate a person than it is to hate a faceless corporation.

Find Passion Points

What topics are people in your target group really, truly passionate about and interested in? Content should be focused around what excites your audience that is related to your product. If you are a camera company, your target is interested in taking better pictures and preserving memories. They are not that interested in your actual camera – they are interested in taking better pictures.

Find something that relates to your brand that really is a passion point (positive or negative) and use that to build equity and connect with people. When I was running marketing for the photography site, we were focused on photographers who were trying to make money on their photography. We found that this group was very passionate about the protection of their copyright, so we regularly shared information and wrote blog posts on this topic and received upwards of 20 comments on some of our posts.

If you are selling energy bars or nutritional supplements there are probably only a few hard-core people who want to talk about the products and the ingredients. These people also, more likely than not, have an interest in fitness and nutrition. Talking about fitness and nutrition perks their interest and positions you as a brand that is concerned about health versus just trying to make a buck selling a product. This is what truly drives brand equity and positive perceptions of your business.

If you are selling fashionable clothing, you may be able to develop some interest by showcasing your new items, but you could probably get more interest by focusing on a passion point – trends and fashion. Share the latest fashion trends, dos and don'ts for looking good or tips and tricks for putting outfits together. By sharing a passion item – fashion trends – you build strong equity for your brand and a strong shared connection.

Again, the key is to relate back to the passion point or interest. To find the passion points, you can listen to what your target audience is already talking about online, or do some targeted focus groups.

Additionally, **focusing on the benefit of your product versus the features will help you get at the passion point.** For example, the energy bar has a number of features (low calorie, lots of energy), but the reason people use it is for the benefit – losing weight or getting in shape. In the case of the clothes company, the feature is the clothes, fabric, where it is made, etc., but the benefit is looking hot and stylish. Think about the benefits that people are trying to get from using your product and this will help you create a relevant content plan.

Provide Something of Value

The best way to connect with current or future consumers is to provide them with something of value. Be a resource for information they are seeking related to your category. One of the main reasons people go online is to look for information. Build an audience through social media by providing useful, relevant and helpful information related to your product or service.

73% of shoppers in the US say that social media directly influenced their purchases. Consumers have the choice of connecting with your brand on social sites. They choose to follow, fan, friend or like you. If you want them to connect with you, you have to provide them with something that is inherently valuable – *your content*. 70% of companies are planning to increase their budgets for off-site social networks, such as Facebook and Twitter[30]. Therefore, the content in your social media-marketing plan needs to stand out from the 70% of companies also joining the network.

In a keynote presentation I gave at a trade show a few months ago, there was a gentleman who was selling health insurance to small and medium-sized businesses. He told me that he struggled with social media because he didn't think that it was really selling. It was about sharing information, which (according to him) doesn't sell. He said that he was currently "selling" by purchasing email lists and sending targeted emails with offers for free sports tickets if they booked a sales call. I asked him how many appointments he got from this. He said none. Apparently *actually selling* wasn't selling anything anyway.

Health insurance is an area that businesses have a lot of questions about. There are so many different packages and factors to consider, and there isn't a lot of flexibility. Many small businesses need help understanding the process and packages and ultimately, would like to talk to someone who can offer them great insurance at a great price. Rather than offering irrelevant sporting tickets, he should be a resource for small businesses looking for information on health insurance plans.

He could create content around what parts of an insurance plan can be cut and aren't heavily used by employees and what are the must-haves. He can help businesses understand the different terms. He could provide recommendations about the best insurance plans for single people versus

30 http://econsultancy.com/reports/marketing-budgets-2010

older people versus people with families. By being a resource and show-ing that he has the best interests of the small business owner at heart, he would come across as a helpful resource instead of as a sleazy sales guy with sports tickets.

Be the Authority

In addition to being useful, many businesses have the opportunity to position themselves as the experts or authority in their chosen field. Most businesses have expert knowledge or resources in an area related to their business and leveraging this in social media could be the perfect way to develop a content plan. Social media is a great way to raise awareness for your expertise by generating and sharing relevant content.

Sharing knowledge and perspectives on relevant industry content posi-tions your business as the expert or authority. For example, there are a few people who I follow on Twitter who consistently tweet really interesting articles about mobile technology. They don't write the articles themselves, they just share the most interesting articles that they come across each day. Simply by sharing useful and interesting links about mobile technologies, I perceive them to be experts on mobile technologies. If I had questions related to mobile technology, I would go to them. If they have businesses related to mobile technology, I would immediately have a certain level or trust and interest because I perceive them to be knowledgeable experts.

Another route to become the expert or authority is to leverage internal resources that have specific knowledge areas. Leveraging the internal ex-perts in your organization can make the difference in a potential customer choosing you over your competition.

For example, I worked with a company that was in the food products in-dustry. Their product had a premium price, but a lot of science went into the nutrition behind it. The company had an entire Research and Development department and a number of doctors and nutritionists on staff.

Many consumers would be surprised to know just how much thought goes in to the nutrition behind the product, and would also be surprised to know that the company employs such a wide range of experts. We created a content plan for the company that centered on sharing their expertise in nutrition with consumers. We developed a unique angle that differentiated them from their competition and leveraged their internal experts to position the brand as a leader in nutrition and health through expert content.

When sharing expert knowledge, some people worry about giving away too much - especially businesses that are in the knowledge industry like accountants, consultants and coaches.

If you share your knowledge and expertise openly will people still pay you? Will they learn how to do it themselves and not hire you? The reality is that there is a much different consumer who wants to invest time in learning from unstructured free online resources and one who will invest in a structured learning program, or pay someone to do it. For example, I could hypothetically do my own taxes (I actually have a finance designation) but it isn't worth the time it would take me to learn everything, plus there is the risk of making mistakes. I may, however, choose to run my own bookkeeping. An accountant sharing small business accounting and tax saving tips could earn my trust and business by sharing expert tips that save me money. When tax time rolls around he would be my go-to resource for tax preparation.

Sharing expert knowledge works well for positioning premium priced services or building positive brand equity.

Reason to Believe

One of the keys to building a compelling content plan is a clear understanding of your reason to believe. Your reason to believe is what will help develop compelling positioning for your brand.

Reason to believe, in this case, refers to whether or not consumers believe that you should be sharing content in this area. Is your content area in line with your positioning and business line? Do you have a background that legitimizes the content area?

For example, if I created a content plan sharing legal advice, people probably wouldn't take it very seriously. I don't have a legal background and I am not a lawyer. People who saw my content would probably not see it as being credible. On the other hand, writing about marketing or, more specifically, social media marketing, is appropriate. I have worked with hundreds of businesses on their marketing and social media strategies, so people reading my content will see it as appropriate and valid that I write about marketing. They have a reason to believe that I am an authority.

The key to choosing your content area is to select a unique and relevant area where you clearly have a reason to be contributing expert content.

It should make sense that the content you post is coming from your business. I don't expect my accountant to share marriage tips. Don't let your content stray too far from what you actually do.

Imagine if McDonald's started a social media strategy around health? Sure, they have launched some new healthy products like apple dippers, but they are not really considered a health expert or advocate. McDonald's doesn't have a reason to believe in the health space, although their public relations department may wish that they could.

Remember, there is LOTS of content out there and not a lot of readers of the content. A successful content strategy requires a reason for people to believe you in a specific content area.

Focus on Solutions

Nobody cares about your product. Write that down. Sure, some people (maybe your family or close friends) might inherently care deeply about your product, but most people are more concerned about a problem and finding a solution for that problem.

Brands are starting to show an understanding of this in how they develop their website content.

People don't really care about Tide laundry detergent, they care about clean clothes. At www.tide.com, a stain finder shows consumers how to get stains out of their clothes. This is solution-focused content. The key when creating solution-focused content is to be sure that you are actually providing an unbiased solution. If the Tide stain finder recommends Tide for every stain, they will lose credibility with their audience. Be open and transparent – if the resource is 100 Ways to Use Tide, call it that. If it is a stain solution resource, provide the best solutions without a bias towards your product. This builds trust and positive equity for your brand, and it positions you as being the most knowledgeable resource for stains.

Focus your marketing efforts on helping your target audience find a solution to their problem. Be unbiased and act as a real resource. Focusing on helping people find solutions builds trust, positive equity and ultimately drives sales.

At the photography startup, we created our content plan based on finding solutions for our target audience. Our target audience of amateur photographers was really interested in creating a business for their photography. They were looking for ways to build a small part-time business for themselves. We shared information on pricing photography and marketing your photography business on blogs and Twitter accounts. We focused our content in helping them solve a real problem – starting a business versus recommending our product. This is what made our blog instantly popular. We had a content plan that surrounded a solution for a problem.

Why will they care?

The final question to ask yourself when creating your content plan is, "Why will they care?" Why will an average person in your target audience care about the content you are producing or sharing? What is in it for them? What do they get out of it?

Always run your content through this final filter. What are you creating that is adding value for your audience? This helps differentiate content that is moderately interesting from content that people care about. Moderately interesting won't cut it in a content cluttered world. To grab attention you need to have great content.

Posting photos from your office or talking about your business strategy doesn't really have a lot of value for most people. I've seen a lot of big brands create entire blogs focused around boring PR topics.

For example, Molson, a beer company, has an entire blog called "Molson in the Community"[31] where they talk about their community outreach. I can see how PR people thought this was a good idea. *They* want to tell *you* about all the great community work they do. But why do *you* want to hear about it? Maybe every now and again it would be nice to know, but certainly very few people are going to read regular blog posts on the topic. The blog has very few comments and very little traffic.

---

31 http://blog.molson.com/community/

Content that Spreads – The Tipping Point

Creating content that spreads is important to a successful content strategy. Chapter 8 on Sharing covers key tools and strategies that can be used to share content on the web. But the tools are only part of it. The real question is how to create content that people want to share with their friends or followers.

In the book *The Tipping Point*[32] Malcolm Gladwell identifies the three components of successful spread of messages – **who** is spreading it, **what** the message is and **the environment** for the message to travel in.

Who are the right people to spread your message or share your content and what are their motivations for sharing? Gladwell identified three types of sharers – the connectors, the mavens and the salespeople. Each of these groups has different reasons for spreading messages. His "Law of the Few" states that you don't need a lot of people to spread your message for it to stick – you just need the right people. Wikipedia summarizes the three types of "spreaders"[33]:

> Connectors are the people who "link us up with the world ... people with a special gift for bringing the world together." They are "a handful of people with a truly extraordinary knack [... for] making friends and acquaintances." He characterizes these individuals as having social networks of over one hundred people. Gladwell attributes the social success of Connectors to "their ability to span many different worlds [... as] a function of something intrinsic to their personality, some combination of curiosity, self-confidence, sociability, and energy."
>
> Mavens are "information specialists", or "people we rely upon to connect us with new information." They accumulate knowledge, especially about the marketplace, and know how to share it with others. A Maven is someone who wants to solve other people's problems, generally by solving his own. According to Gladwell, Mavens start "word-of-mouth epidemics" due to their knowledge, social skills,

---

32 http://www.gladwell.com/tippingpoint/index.html

33 http://en.wikipedia.org/wiki/The_Tipping_Point

and ability to communicate. As Gladwell states, "Mavens are really information brokers, sharing and trading what they know."

Salesmen are "persuaders", charismatic people with powerful negotiation skills. They tend to have an indefinable trait that goes beyond what they say, which makes others want to agree with them.

The next component for a message to spread is the content of the message itself. This is what Gladwell identifies as "The Stickiness Factor." Whatever in a message makes it stick in someone's memory is its Stickiness Factor.

Finally, the "Power of Context" states that their environment affects how humans behave. As Gladwell says, "Epidemics are sensitive to the conditions and circumstances of the times and places in which they occur." For social media marketing the "context" is the sites or tools that are most appropriate for your message.

For your content plan consider WHO can help spread your content, WHAT type of content is most naturally sharable and which TOOLS or ENVIRONMENT make the content most likely to be shared.

Key Questions in Creating your Content Plan:

The key questions to ask yourself about your content plan are:

1) Who do you want to talk to?

Your marketing objectives and your target audience determine this.

2) What do you want to talk to them about?

What content do you want to share with them? How does the content link back to your product and marketing objectives?

3) Why will they care?

Will they really care? Does your content really solve a problem, hit a passion point or provide a resource? Is it really just about you?

4)   How will you engage them?

How will you actually engage them? This is where the directions of the Social Media Field Guide come in to play.

ACTION ITEMS AND KEY LEARNINGS

CHAPTER 7:

Publishing

The first direction in The Social Media Field Guide is publishing. Publishing can be a very powerful social media marketing strategy when used correctly. Publishing as a social media marketing strategy means to create your own content for your audience. This could take the form of a blog (a type of website that you can create), a podcast (audio or video that you upload and share regularly), a webinar (an online presentation), an e-book (an electronic-only book), and email newsletter or a white paper (a thought piece on an issue or idea).

A publishing strategy means that you are actually creating – writing or recording – your own original material and publishing it online. Publishing content allows companies to develop an audience and connect with target consumers based on an interest or information need that relates to the product that they sell.

For example, a high-end coffee shop owner may create a web video explaining the different types of coffee beans or the secrets to brewing a perfect cup of coffee. The coffee shop owner is creating and publishing web content (blogs, videos, webinars, etc.) based on content that their target audience is interested in as a way to establish a relationship with the target audience.

The focus of the content is not on the coffee shop itself, but on a subject that the target audience *(coffee lovers)* is passionate about *(coffee beans and brewing)*.

Publishing can allow you to connect with your target by sharing useful and relevant information and demonstrating that you **know** your product category better than anyone else (and therefore your product is awesome). Scott's Miracle Grow has a number of blogs[5] on lawn care managed by grass experts who help you solve your grass problems. In their publishing strategy, Scott's publishes different blogs on how to care for your lawn. The blog content – *lawn care* – is clearly relevant to the target audience – *those willing to invest in caring for their lawn*. The blog does not overtly sell or recommend Scott's products; it focuses on how to effectively care for your lawn, prevent problems and find solutions.

Publishing this content serves a number of marketing objectives for Scott's. First, it enables them to build equity as "the lawn experts" by showing their vast knowledge on grass and lawn care. By showcasing their knowledge and expertise on lawn care (hey – they even have scientists who work there), consumers assume that their products also reflect this knowledge (after all, they have scientists who work there). Second, they can attract new customers who may search online for lawn care tips and find the Scott's blog. This awareness could then lead to an investment in Scott's products. Third, Scott's is building a trusted relationship with their audience as a partner in lawn care. Rather than just selling lawn products, they are positioning themselves as a trusted resource in their area. When selling a premium product, building equity and trust are vital to commanding a premium price.

The key to successful publishing is to create content that your target audience is truly interested in and resist the urge to sell your product blatently. By providing valuable content to your target audience, you can build credibility, equity, and trust while ultimately building relationships that create new customers, increase loyalty and provide positive recommendations from existing customers.

Linking to Your Marketing Objectives

When looking at publishing as a strategic social media marketing tool, it is important to consider your marketing goals and objectives. A clear understanding of your marketing goals will help you determine the right type of content to create based on the audience you are trying to reach. Once the content is determined, you can assess whether or not publishing is the right tool to achieve your goals.

One of the advantages of publishing content as a part of your social media marketing strategy is that it can achieve a wide variety of marketing goals and objectives.

Everyone is a Publisher

"Publisher" used to be a term restricted to those who produced magazines, newspapers and books. But with the tools available on the web, anyone can become a publisher without spending a penny. Perhaps one of the greatest changes to have taken place on the web over the past ten years is the ease at which average people can create and publish content online. Ten years ago, if you wanted to make a website you would probably have to hire a programmer and a designer and know your way

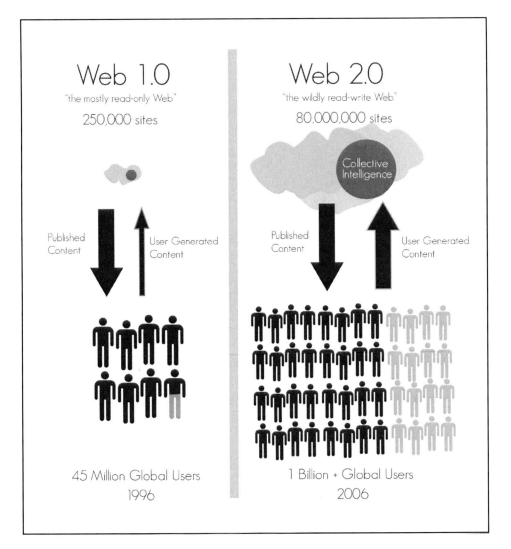

around HTML coding. It was time consuming, costly and not very flexible. Only the experts had the access and ability to create or change the content. Updating your website often meant waiting for a webmaster to implement your changes – costing you time and money.

Today you can create your own website in about 10 minutes with site builders like Google Sites or EditSpot – no programming knowledge required. Not only is it simple to create a website, but it is also easier than ever to edit websites. Even big corporate websites are built on some sort of Content Management Systen (CMS) that allows average users with no programming knowledge to easily edit the site content.

In addition to creating and editing websites, average people can now create blogs, audio podcasts or video podcasts (these are explained in more detail later in the chapter).

The web has changed from a read web – where you would go to the Internet primarily to consume content and information – to a read-write web – where you can both read information as well as create it. Rather than passively consuming information, you can create and interact with content. This is what the term "Web 2.0" is all about.

Today, anyone can be a publisher and create a website, blog, podcast or video in less than an hour, with minimal (if any) monitary investment required.

Content Clutter

With publishing tools so accessible, everyone is a publisher and there are millions of blogs, websites and podcasts published. There is a proliferation of content online and even the best quality content has difficulty standing out and building an audience.

There are over 160 million blogs and about 329 million blog readers in the US, each of whom read about 3 blogs.[34]

Over 88% of businesses are now active on social media, which means that the competition for attention is higher than ever.

This sets a higher bar for publishers or content creators. In addition to creating interesting and relevant content to publish, part of your strategy must include how to build an audience for your content and where to syndicate it online. The good news is that many of the social media tools that we cover in this book (Facebook, Twitter, social news sites, etc.) are excellent syndication platforms for your content.

In addition to leveraging social media to build an audience for your content, consider how you can connect your current customers, direct mail subscribers, email newsletter readers, etc., to your content. Look for opportunities to promote your content with your existing customer or

34 http://www.jeffbullas.com/2012/08/02/
   blogging-statistics-facts-and-figures-in-2012-infographic/

client base – in your physical store, through signs or with cards that you give to customers.

Content Strategy

"If you want us to talk to you, tell us something. Make it something interesting for a change." - Cluetrain Manifesto[10]

If you want to create content as a way to engage with your audience, the *key* question to ask yourself is "What subject areas is my target audience *really* interested in?"

I have mentioned previously the photography blog I ran that regularly received over 20 comments on blog posts and generated high-quality users for our website. We almost never talked about our company or products – we talked about what photographers were interested in: the business of photography.

In addition to understanding our target audience, we knew we needed to stand out. With all of the existing blogs giving photographers tips, we needed a strategy that would set us apart. We leveraged internal and external experts to create content that photographers couldn't get anywhere else. As someone with a lot of marketing and branding experience, I wrote blog posts on photography marketing techniques and how to sell and price photography. This was unique content because many photographers do not have any marketing training. In addition, we had a lawyer write weekly posts on issues surrounding photography laws. This column was especially popular because many photographers in our target audience had legal questions about selling their photography. What was particularly valuable to our audience was that they could ask questions through the comments section and get answers to their questions.

Our blog was providing content that was of interest to our target audience from experts within our company.

This content strategy achieved a number of marketing objectives. First, it helped us to acquire new users for our website; they were drawn to our great content and were then interested in learning more about our services. Second, it branded us as a company that knew and understood the needs of the amateur photographer who was trying to start a business. Third, it drove loyalty and advocacy as we were able to develop real relationships with some of our most loyal users. Finally, it built equity for our website as a brand that was an expert and thought leader in the area.

A strong content strategy should provide interesting and valuable content to your target audience while meeting your marketing and business objectives.

One additional key consideration in developing a publishing strategy is to overcome the fear of being niche. Many companies don't want to pigeonhole themselves into a small and specific niche of content that they will cover. With the proliferation of content, the best strategy to building an audience is to be as niche and specific as possible.

In his book *The Long Tail*[9], Chris Anderson discusses how the web has created large opportunities for "Long Tail" content. The Long Tail is the small niche content that drives smaller audiences versus the generic "best sellers". For example, *TheNew York Times*, which produces generic news content with broad mass appeal, would not be in the Long Tail, whereas a small locally-focused newspaper or a newspaper focused on industry-specific news and updates would be in the Long Tail. What the evolution of the web has showed us is that there are consumers looking for that very specific Long Tail content, and with content publishing costs so low and national audiences with an interest in your niche, content can be more easily developed. The future of publishing and content creation lies in serving niche markets effectively on a large scale.

Don't be afraid to make your content niche and specific. There is an audience for everything.

Selecting Publishing Tools

If publishing is the right direction for your social media marketing strategy, target audience and content, the next step is to select the publishing tool that is the best fit for your content. Some content is better communicated through text, others video, some through audio and others through in-depth e-books or white papers.

The major publishing tools include:

- Blogs
- Podcasts
- Webinars

- Ebooks and White Papers

- Videos

Answer the following questions to help select the most relevant publishing tool:

- How regularly do I plan on producing content?

- Is my content best communicated verbally, aurally or visually?

- Do I have internal resources to develop the content or would I need to rely on guests?

- Do I have "personalities" internally that can produce the content?

- How much time can I commit to developing the content?

- Do I have the required A/V equipment?

Answering these questions will help determine the right publishing strategy for your business.

PUBLISHING TOOLS:
Blogs

What is a Blog?

If you are active online you have probably heard of blogs, but what exactly is a blog? According to Wikipedia:

"A **blog** is a type of website, usually maintained by an individual with regular entries of commentary, descriptions of events, or other material such as graphics or video. Entries are commonly displayed in reverse-chronological order. "Blog" can also be used as a verb, meaning *to maintain or add content to a blog.*"[11]

A blog is essentially a type of website that has regular updates (or blog posts) where the newest or most recent updates are displayed first. Blogs also typically allow readers to leave comments and respond to the blog posts. One of the main appeals of blogs is how easily they can be set up. A blog can be created for free in under an hour using a site like Wordpress[12] or Blogger[13] with no technical or programming knowledge required.

You can see the Boot Camp Digital blog at www.bootcampdigital.com/blog or in the screenshot.

Since blogs are relatively easy to create, there are many of them - over 126 million[35] bloggers (people who write blogs) write on a variety of topics from personal experience subjects like family, children, parenting and single living to professional topics like marketing, business and politics. Blogs can be found on nearly any topic – from how to manage your lawn to quilting to dealing with autistic children to concrete and construction.

Blogs can be created for both personal and professional reasons. On the personal side, many bloggers create blogs about subjects they are interested in or an issue that they are dealing with – like surviving cancer, photography, blogging as a pet or living with depression. On a professional side, blogs are used by individuals to position themselves as experts and share their knowledge about their given profession. Companies also use blogs to position themselves as experts in their field and share knowledge

---

35 http://royal.pingdom.com/2010/01/22/internet-2009-in-numbers/

and information with their users or talk about topics that their audience is passionate about.

How to Set Up a Blog

When creating a blog, the technology or actually creating the blog is the easy part. As mentioned above, a starter blog can be created on www.wordpress.com or www.blogger.com. Businesses that are serious about blogging can add a blog to their website, usually for relatively little cost. The difficult part of blogging is creating a compelling and relevant subject area for your blog, using effective blog writing and revising over time based on feedback and responses from your readers.

How Are Companies Using Blogs?

Corporate blogs have had mixed success over the years. While there are many extremely successful corporate blogs, there are probably even more failures. Many corporate blogs fail because companies fail to develop interesting content or do not regularly update the content. When considering a blog for business purposes, content should be updated at least once a week (ideally 3 - 5 posts per week) and an average blog post can take about an hour to write.

The *key* to creating a successful corporate blog is what lies in the middle of the Social Media Field Guide Compass – **content**. Compelling and interesting content is *vital* to the success of a blog (see Chapter 6 – Content). Prior to creating a blog, spend time developing a clear content plan – who will write what and when – including content that will be of value to your target audience. Many companies use their blogs as an additional PR tool where they tout the latest and greatest achievements of the company. Instead of focusing on what *you* want to talk about, focus on what your *target* is actually interested in.

Blogging Example:

Zappos CEO Blog

Zappos is a company that sells shoes and clothing online. Zappos is well known for their quirky corporate culture and outstanding customer service. Zappos runs a number of very successful blogs.

One of the more interesting blogs is the Zappos CEO blog. On the Zappos CEO blog[8], the Zappos CEO Tony Hsieh shares his insights and thoughts on the company in an informal and honest way. When Zappos was acquired by Amazon he shared his thoughts. His open and personable style brings credibility, authenticity and transparency to the subject that would not be possible in a standard press release. Tony's openness is obvious in this excerpt from the blog post:

> **Probably the biggest question I've gotten lately has been "How's the Amazon acquisition been? How have things changed?"**
>
> The truth is, there have been a couple of minor annoyances. We're now part of a public company, so moving forward, we aren't able to disclose our financial numbers as freely as we were able to do before (but that would have happened anyway had we gone public on our own). We also have more travel restrictions for various legal and tax reasons.
>
> On the flip side though, we've retained our independence and our culture is as strong as before the acquisition. We've been learning a lot from each other and the new partnership has enabled us to move even faster towards the Zappos vision of delivering happiness to the world."

The Zappos CEO blog is honest, transparent and authentic, and as a result, readers feel that they are making a connection with Tony and the company. The blog provides an outlet for existing fans and customers to get real updates on the company in addition to building loyalty and positive equity for Zappos.

Blogging Example:

Marriott CEO Blog[36]

The CEO of Marriott International started a blog in 2007 – he saw it as a good way to communicate with both internal and external stakeholders. He was one of the early adopters in corporate CEO blogs (the blog can still be seen at www. blogs.marriott.com[37]). The blog is called "Marriott on the Move" and includes images and posts on a wide variety of topics.

According to chief executive Bill Marriott, "That's the importance of public relations, of advertising, of everything we do," Marriott said. "And this is just another channel." Marriott also likes how the blog shows that he is "a human just like everybody else." He sometimes breaks from writing about corporate issues to post about the movies he sees on Saturdays with his wife.

Marriott has thousands of employees around the world, who make up about one-fifth of the blog's readership and comment frequently. "It is the virtual substitute for Bill Marriott visiting every hotel," Matthews said.

One year after the launch, the blog averaged about 6,000 visitors per week and had more than 600,000 total visitors since its inception in January 2007.

What is more, in addition to the less tangible results mentioned above, Marriott has made more than $5 million in bookings from people who clicked through to the reservation page from Marriott's blog. Marriott has seen results both through direct and traceable sales as well as intangible benefits of personalizing and humanizing the company.

---

36 http://www.washingtonpost.com/wp-dyn/content/article/2008/08/24/ AR2008082401517_2.html?hpid=topnews

37 http://www.blogs.marriott.com/

Blogging Example:

Small Business – Dolcezza Gelato[38]

Blogging isn't just for big businesses – small businesses can get big returns on blogging. "It's a small business, so we don't have a marketing budget," said Robb Duncan, who began a blog[39] for his Georgetown gelato shop, Dolcezza, about two years ago. "We've never done any ads or promoting because we can't afford it. So I guess it's kind of guerrilla marketing, and it's free."

Sure, blogging may not have a direct financial cost, but it does take time. The good news is that in most retail and restaurant small businesses there are a variety of underutilized resources that aren't as busy during slow times.

The results from blogging have been powerful for this small niche store. When their second store opened in July of 2008, Duncan used the blog to advertise an opening night ice cream giveaway. Generating "buzz" about a new promotion can be difficult for small businesses and the blog was an easy way to get the message out. He ended up serving over 300 gallons of ice cream to more than 1,000 customers that night – all through word of mouth generated from the blog.

Blogs are the HUB of an Online and Social Marketing Strategy

A blog is typically viewed as the hub of an online or social media marketing strategy. Since a blog is typically hosted on the main website for a business (eg., www.bootcampdigital.com/blog) it drives traffic back to the main website, where a variety of calls to action can be used to convert website visitors into customers.

Many businesses view their blog as the hub of their social media activity. They use social networks and sharing sites to build an audience and

---

38 http://www.washingtonpost.com/wp-dyn/content/article/2008/08/24/
    AR2008082401517_2.html?hpid=topnews

39 http://www.gelato-ology.blogspot.com/

connect with customers, but their ultimate goal is to display thought leadership and drive consumers back to their blog.

Typically a blog fits with internet marketing in the following way: A company writes a blog post that builds their brand positioning and is interesting to the target audience. The post is then shared through Facebook, Twitter, Linkedin, discussion forums, etc. As people read the interesting post, they share it with their friends and perhaps click on a call to action on the site, like signing up for a newsletter or downloading an eBook.

A blog is usually considered one of the most powerful and necessary tools in a social media marketing toolkit. In addition to sharing thought leadership and building brand equity, it serves as a marketing hub and makes other social media sites like Facebook and LinkedIn more effective.

PUBLISHING TOOLS:
Podcasts

Podcasts are another popular form of publishing. A few years ago there was a lot of interest in podcasts, but over time, businesses have found them difficult to maintain, and only a small segment of the population listens to podcasts. That being said, for some businesses they may still represent an opportunity, and they are worth understanding.

A podcast is a video or audio recording that happens with some regularity (e.g., weekly or biweekly), similar to a radio show. Also, like a TV or Radio Show, a podcast will typically have a theme and a name, like This Week in Photography or the Digg Nation Podcast. Each weekly episode fits within the theme of the overall podcast.

The difference between a podcast and a radio show is anyone can create and publish a podcast and it can be listened to online, on-demand at any time. Podcasts are often not streamed live – they are recorded and published online. Podcasts can also be syndicated online through iTunes, where people can subscribe to a podcast and have each new episode downloaded.

A podcast can be a strategic part of your marketing mix, but it requires a regular commitment to creating content. Since a podcast is like a radio or TV show, a podcast should have a general theme and regular episodes. When creating a podcast, selecting a theme that is both relevant to your target audience and marketing objectives is vital. After the theme is created, filling the podcast with entertaining episodes generally requires a content calendar. One of the advantages of podcasts is that guests can be included to keep content fresh and interesting.

A podcast can be an effective marketing tool if you have enough content to regularly fill a 10 – 30 minute time period with audio or video. Podcasts work well in industries that are constantly changing and where people have a strong desire to stay up-to-date or educated.

How Are Companies Using Podcasts?

Corporate use of podcasts is limited; however, as video and audio production costs have gone down, they are becoming more popular. Many businesses use podcasts to demonstrate thought leadership or expert knowledge in their given fields. Podcasts are especially relevant in industries where consumers are looking for a lot of information or are in highly technical fields.

Podcasting Example: Tellabs[40]

Tellabs provides telecommunications solutions to telecom service providers by enabling them to deliver voice, video and data services over wired and wireless networks.

The telecom industry is highly competitive, and Tellabs wanted to cut through the noise and change their image. They launched a podcast called "Get Schooled" on their Inspire the New Life Website. The goal of the podcast was to provide customers and industry personel information on the latest products and technical leadership from Tellabs.

The podcasts generated tens of thousands of views, which is considerable given the size and nature of telecommunications. In addition, the company landed an interview with the head of telecom research for Reuters and won a MarCom Platinum Creative Award. While sales attributed to the podcast have not been disclosed, the industry awareness and brand equity met the marketing objectives of the program. "We wanted to be able to deliver messages in a more dynamic and interactive manner and other means that

---

40 http://www.marketingprofs.com/casestudy/93

Tellabs supports. This gives Tellabs an early opportunity to impress our thoughts on that targeted audience," said Mark O'Malley, Director of External Marketing for Tellabs.

PUBLISHING TOOLS:
Webinars

Webinars and teleseminars are increasing in their use and importance as a part of a marketing mix. A webinar or teleseminar is a live event where listeners will call in to a conference call line and possibly watch a slide presentation or live-stream video online. Webinars are usually pre-scheduled and run 30 minutes to an hour in length on a given topic. People who want to call in to a webinar will usually provide their email address to register for the webinar in advance. Webinars can be free, but some companies charge a fee to attend their webinars.

Webinars are still relatively new in the social media marketing toolbox. Up until a few years ago, webinar software was expensive and unreliable for large numbers of participants. Webinar technology has evolved over the past few years making it a simple, low-cost marketing tool.

Webinars are a very effective marketing tool for building relationships and positioning your brand or company as the experts in your field. As the Social Media Field Guide shows, *content* is the key to success in any social media marketing strategy, but this is especially true for webinars.

Webinars are typically educational in content since they require a fairly lengthy time commitment. The webinar can include internal people at your company providing education or experts from the industry. For example, a design agency hired me to give a webinar on social media marketing because they knew their audience (medium-sized businesses) was interested in social media. The webinar was only made available to their current clients as a reward for being a valued client.

In addition to using webinars with existing clients, webinars are an extremely attractive lead generation tool. Most webinars require participants to provide their email address to participate. This helps businesses to develop email lists of targeted potential clients and convert them into customers over time. Taking this a step further, prior to registering for the webinar, a number of lead qualification questions can be asked (e.g., are you planning on buying a car in the next year, how big is your company, are you a decision maker, etc.) and the information can be passed along to sales teams. Keep in mind that making a sale or getting a new customer is a process – the sale does not usually happen immediately. By acquiring an email address, you can begin to build a relationship or send marketing messages that will eventually lead to a sale.

One additional note about webinars is that they are extremely effective marketing tools for B-to-B (Business to Business) social media marketing. Since B-to-B marketing involves business professionals who are often education-oriented, webinars can provide a simple, low-cost way to provide education to current or future customers and also to generate leads.

How to Set Up a Webinar

Webinars are relatively easy to set up and run. There are a number of low-cost webinar sites like www.gotowebinar.com or www.webex.com where for about $100 a month you can create a webinar with multiple participants. A webinar can be created in about 10 minutes with a simple user interface. All you need to do is select your topic and promote the webinar. Most webinar solutions will provide you with email lists of all of the participants and you can add survey questions at the beginning and end of the webinar.

Example:

Hubspot Webinars

Hubspot is an example of using publishing technologies to generate leads and acquire new customers. Hubspot is a provider of "Inbound Marketing Software" that helps businesses grow traffic, generate leads and drive sales. Their target audience is marketing professionals.

Hubspot runs webinars[6] on Internet marketing topics like social media or lead generation tactics that are generally of interest to their audience. Hubspot's webinar topics vary from showcasing their internal talent and findings to running webinars with best selling authors. Last year, I joined a Hubspot webinar with David Meerman Scott, author of *The New Rules of PR and Marketing* (definitely worth a read if you get a chance to pick it up). Once the webinar subject is selected, Hubspot uses their other social media channels to promote the webinar. People who are interested in Internet marketing register for the webinar, provide their email address and a respond to a few questions (used for lead qualification).

During the webinar, Hubspot will briefly (typically under two minutes) provide product information and how to get more information. After the webinar, the email addresses are fed into the Hubspot marketing database and the participants are scored for lead generation based on the survey questions. The best potential customers may be contacted by a sales representative.

By creating interesting and compelling webinar content, Hubspot is able to generate brand awareness, get leads and ultimately drive sales.

PUBLISHING TOOLS:
E-books and White Papers

E-books and white papers are popular marketing tools for businesses that have a target audience that is interested in education and information.

An e-book (which stands for electronic book and is also called a digital book, ebook or eBook) is defined as "an electronic version of a printed book which can be read on a personal computer or hand-held device designed specifically for this purpose." Since there are no costs to print or distribute an e-book, it is a simple, low-cost way to distribute content online.

According to Wikipedia:

> A white paper is an authoritative report or guide that often addresses issues and how to solve them. White papers are used to educate readers and help people make decisions. They are often used in politics, business, and technical fields. In commercial use, the term "white paper" (or "whitepaper") has also come to refer to documents used by businesses as a marketing or sales tool.[41]

---

41 http://en.wikipedia.org/wiki/White_paper

E-books and white papers are popular marketing strategies because they have high perceived value to the recipients and typically require an email address and other information to download. An "e-book" or a "white paper" sounds (and ideally *is*) much more valuable than a handful of blog posts, even though the two may take the same amount of time.

One of the key differences is that e-books and white papers are often purchased, whereas blog posts and podcasts are usually free. If publishing is already a part of your strategic marketing plan through blogging or podcasts, repurposing (a fancy word for reworking and reusing) the content into a free e-book or white paper could be a good social media marketing strategy. The *key* to repurposing content for e-books or white papers is to make sure that your coverage of the subject is thorough, well organized and valuable enough that a downloader sees real benefit in them.

Similar to webinars, e-books and white papers can be used strategically to attain email addresses for email marketing or lead generation and qualification. Typically, in order to "download your free white paper," you have to provide your email address and potentially some additional information. E-books and whitepapers are also often used without requiring an email address and simply given away for free as a tool to demonstrate brand equity and thought leadership.

Ebooks and white papers are also often used as a part of a PR campaign. If the content includes original research or data based on user data or surveys, it can actually generate press from bloggers and traditional media. When producing an e-book or white paper, consider leveraging PR (see Chapter 13 on social media PR) if the content is truly unique and new. This can provide additional reach for your message.

E-books and white papers are primarily used by B-to-B marketers. However, there is also potential for these tools in the consumer market. For example, if you run a bicycle shop (I recently purchased a new road bike) you could publish a white paper on how to size yourself for a bike, a beginner's guide to cyclist lingo, road bicycling etiquette or 10 bike riding tips for new riders. Both of these white paper strategies would be best suited for new beginner cyclists. If you are looking to connect with seasoned riders, the white papers could contain more advanced topics. The key is to find the most relevant content for your marketing goals and target audience and put it into a clear and useful format of either a white paper or e-book.

How to Create E-books and White Papers

On the technical side, to create e-books and white papers all you need is word-processing software and a way for people to sign up to receive your e-book on your website. The content is simply emailed – typically in the form of a PDF to prevent duplication or alteration. On the creative side, e-books and white papers require interesting and compelling content.

First, the subject area needs to be interesting enough that a consumer is willing to provide their email address to get the content. If the content is extremely basic, they may just look for another blog post or news article covering the subject. Second, the content itself should be thorough and long enough that it seems worth the effort. Typically, white papers and e-books range in length from 5 to 20 pages. The content of the white paper should showcase your knowledge on the subject and position your company as experts in the area.

PUBLISHING TOOLS:
Videos

Video sharing has increased in popularity over the past few years as the cost to purchase video recording and editing equipment has decreased. For about a hundred dollars you can buy a low cost camcorder and start recording videos. Most computers today come with video editing software built in and it is remarkably easy to add graphics and music to videos.

There are a large number of free video sharing sites. A video sharing site is a website where a video can be uploaded and made publicly available for people to watch directly from their web browsers like YouTube.com. Posting videos on YouTube is entirely free and you can create your own business "channel."

Video is a very popular medium because it has the opportunity to create a stronger connection with consumers. Think about the difference in the level of connection if you read an article written by me versus watching a video. The content in both may be the same, but by watching me in a video, you get a sense of who I am and my personality. Video marketing helps build emotional connections.

Video Marketing

The key to successfully leveraging YouTube (or any video site) is to create compelling and interesting videos that your target audience wants to watch. Video is an extremely powerful communication tool – it allows marketers to communicate much more than text or audio alone. Again, the videos that you create should link back to your marketing goals and objectives and a deep understanding of your target audience and what they are interested in.

There are many opportunities for brands and companies to use video to communicate with their audience. The CEO of a company can use video to talk about corporate changes or provide additional perspective to press releases (or press disasters). An advertising agency can create quick videos that show their creative process. A clothing store can create videos of employees showing their favorite items in the store, or modeling new items. An accountant can video tape himself sharing tax tips or comparing small business accounting software. The opportunities are endless.

They *key* is the core of the Social Media Field Guide – content.

If you have an idea for a "funny viral video" think again. There is lots of hysterical content on YouTube, and most businesses don't have the experience to really be funny. The goal of video marketing shouldn't be to create the next viral video. It should be to communicate something relevant, useful or entertaining to your target audience.

In addition to creating your own videos, many companies are encouraging their fans to share videos through contests or by featuring the videos on their website or blog. For the Superbowl, Doritos ran a contest where people submitted commercials and the winning commercial actually ran during the Superbowl.

Even small and less exciting businesses can leverage user-generated videos. A local credit union ran a contest where users submitted videos that incorporated the bank mascot for a chance to win $1,000. The winner was selected based on voting, and many of the contest entrants promoted their videos to their friends and on social networks to get votes and win the prize. This led to increased awareness and exposure for the credit union. Video sharing sites make it easier than ever for brands to run video contests.

In addition to running a contest, companies can encourage their fans to post things like testimonials or show the product in action. By asking customers to send you their videos and featuring the videos on your blog, website or in your newsletter, you cultivate and reward their enthusiasm. These videos can also be used in other marketing, like TV commercials.

YouTube

Youtube is the most popular video-sharing site. According to the YouTube site:

> "Founded in February 2005, YouTube is the world's most popular online video community, allowing millions of people to discover, watch and share originally-created videos.

> YouTube allows people to easily upload and share video clips on www.YouTube.com and across the Internet through websites, mobile devices, blogs, and e-mail.

> Everyone can participate in the YouTube community by watching, sharing, and commenting on videos. People can see first-hand accounts of current events, relive their favorite TV moments, find videos about their hobbies and interests, discover new artists and filmmakers, and even uncover the quirky and unusual.

> As more people capture special moments on video, YouTube is empowering them to share their experiences, talents, and expertise with the world."

> According to YouTube, people are watching 2 billion videos a day on YouTube and uploading hundreds of thousands of videos daily - every minute, 24 hours of video is uploaded to YouTube[42].

Linking video to other social networks

One of the advantages of video sharing sites is that the videos can also be connected to other social networks. For example, a video posted on YouTube can also be embedded on your blog or website, on Facebook or shared on Twitter. Posting a video isn't enough – you must have a clear plan

---

42 http://www.youtube.com/t/fact_sheet

to promote it and drive views of it. Consider how videos can fit with the rest of your social media strategy.

Video Example:

BlendTec YouTube Success

One of the biggest YouTube brand success stories is a high-end blender company called BlendTec[43]. Blendtec is famous for creating a video series called "Will It Blend?"[44]

According to BlendTec CEO Tom Dickson,[45] "For years I've been doing a test where I start the motor and jam a piece of timber into the blades and test the strength of the drive component, the electronics, and the blade itself. We thought it might be fun to try out some other things that people might find amusing." And that is how simply the Will It Blend videos were created. As a part of product testing, they had been blending pieces of timber. They thought it was funny and did a quick recording of it to post online.

The idea for the Will it Blend series happened by accident. The first video was created for only $50. It went live on the company's website on November 2, 2006, and after only one day on the site it received 23,000 hits. The video was then released on YouTube where the views exploded – their "Golf Ball Smoothie" video received over 1.7 million views.

BlendTec's stated initial objective for the Will It Blend videos was increased brand awareness for their line of blenders. "We wanted to demonstrate the power and durability of the Blendtec blender," said CEO Tom Dickson. "Even though we had the best blender in the world, people didn't know who we were." As a result of the campaign, however, their retail sales have increased by over 700% and

---

43 www.blendtec.com

44 www.willitblend.com

45 http://www.wordtracker.com/academy/case-study-willitblend

the Will It Blend series has received many millions of views on YouTube.

Publishing Check-List

Publishing can be a powerful marketing strategy but it requires consistent effort and the ability to create fresh new content. Publishing may be a good strategy for your business if:

- You have unique and interesting knowledge that you can share.

- Your target audience is looking for information.

- You have the capacity to produce regular content (once a week).

- It matches your marketing objectives.

- You can promote the content you are publishing.

ACTION ITEMS AND KEY LEARNINGS

Want to put the Social Media Field Guide into Action?
Go to www.bootcampdigital.com/actionplanner to
download your FREE Field Guide action planner.

CHAPTER 8:

Sharing

Sharing is the next direction in the Social Media Field Guide. Sharing means that you are syndicating (or sharing) content online. The focus here is not so much on creating your own content, but in showing your interest and expertise in an area by sharing unique and relevant content. Sharing is slightly different than publishing in that the goal of publishing is to create in-depth unique content, whereas sharing is more focused on sharing or syndicating content that you have already created or that someone else has created. The goal of online sharing is to publicly share content with a broad audience.

3 Sharing Strategies

There are three unique focus areas for marketers when it comes to sharing: sharing your own content, having others share your content and encouraging others to share their content.

SHARING STRATEGY 1:
Share Your Own Content

The first option in a sharing strategy is to share your own content. The web has made sharing easier than ever. You can share music through sites like Blip.fm, photos through Flickr.com or Instagram, videos through YouTube.com, slideshows and presentations through Slideshare.com, PDF files through Scribd.com, inspiration through Pinterest and so on.

Many businesses or individuals that don't have the time or energy to create their own content will rely on a sharing strategy. This is different from publishing in that publishing focuses more on creating a consistent stream of targeted content (like a podcast or a blog), whereas sharing focuses more on syndicating content that you already have or that you find online. Regardless of your business line, there are many aspects of your business that can create unique sharing opportunities. Sharing your own content is really about finding interesting items pertaining to your brand, business or employees and posting on social sharing sites. For example, if I don't have time to write a blog post, I may share an article from *The New York Times* about social media. Sharing this content still establishes my thought leadership, yet I don't have to do the work of publishing the content myself.

I may also choose to share other content that my organization has created. For example, I recently created a presentation on Social Media for College Students that I shared on Slideshare. I then created a blog post where I embedded the presentation and shared some additional tips. Next I took the blog post and promoted it on Twitter, Facebook and LinkedIn. Sharing is an integrated process

Why sharing your own content matters

As discussed in the Publishing Chapter (Chapter 7), creating or publishing content - even great content - does not guarantee an audience. In the movie *Field of Dreams*, Kevin Costner builds a baseball field in his yard after hearing the whispers, "If you build it, he will come." In social media, "If you build it, nobody will know" – you have to tell them and promote it through sharing and social networks (Social Networks are covered in Chapter 9).

This is why sharing your own content is so important. In the Publishing Chapter (Chapter 7), we discussed the value of creating your own content. However, if your audience can't find your content, you won't receive any of those benefits. They key to an effective publishing strategy is syndication. Sharing sites are one of the key forms of syndicating your content.

In addition to using sharing sites to develop an audience for content created as a publishing strategy, there are also opportunities to share additional content to build connections with your brand. Sharing photos and videos of your products, services, location or employees can help generate awareness and it shows up in search engine results when people search for your company or items related to your company.

SHARING STRATEGY 2:
Have Others Share Your Content

The second sharing strategy is to make your content as sharable as possible and to encourage your audience to pass your content along and help spread the word. How can you encourage people to share your content with their family and friends to increase your reach and the spread of your message? A number of both technical and content driven strategies can be employed to increase the sharability of your content.

On the technical side, we will cover RSS feeds and sharing widgets and on the creative side, we will cover content that spreads and how to encourage sharing.

When publishing or sharing content, it is important you have a plan to encourage people to share your content with others and build viral spread. There is so much content created every day that you need to have a plan to syndicate your content online. One of the key ways to make sure your content draws attention is to encourage others to do the work for you – via sharing. Encouraging and incentivising people to share your content is vital in building an audience and drawing attention to your work. Provide cues for people to share your content and make it as easy as possible.

ENCOURAGE FRIENDS AND FANS TO SHARE THEIR CONTENT:

The third sharing strategy is encouraging others to share content related to your brand. Your brand fans and enthusiasts can share testimonials, photos and videos related to your brand. This is often referred to as User Generated Content (UGC) where average users are generating their own content. Encouraging UGC can be as simple as highlighting customers who share their photos/videos/success stories or running a contest to encourage sharing. The benefit of encouraging fans to share is that it highlights that you do in fact have fans and that they LOVE your brand/product/company.

Fans of brands will post photos, videos and stories about products, companies, brands and experiences. Some of the most common shared content about brands includes:

- **Testimonials** – If your brand really impacts people your users may want to create testimonials about how your product has helped them. Testimonials can include videos, photos of the results (before and after shots), or stories. A friend of mine used an acne product called Proactive and achieved dramatic results. She sent them a quick video about how the product changed her life because she was so passionate about it – they didn't compensate her in any way. The video was then featured in TV commercials for procative.

- **New product uses** – Consumers will sometimes share stories, videos or photos about unique or interesting uses for products. This type of content also has the potential to go viral because it tends to be interesting or amusing.

- **Tutorials** – People like to help people, even when there isn't anything in it for them. Average users have been known to write or record product tutorials or tips for how to use more complicated products. Look up any question regarding how to use an iPhone on YouTube and you'll find thousands of video tutorials created by average users who want to help others.

- **Your product in action** – If your product provides a good visual experience for people, they may share photos and videos that show your product in action. For example, search for a specific camera brand on YouTube and you are likely to find video tutorials of other photographers sharing tips and tricks on how to best use the camera. Most restaurants find their products (meals) are photographed and shared all over social networks.

- **Contest entries** – Over the past few years, a number of brands have run contests requiring people to create and share stories, videos or photos to win contests. A small island in Australia ran a popular contest where they had a job posting for a Dream Job where the winner became the Queensland Island Caretaker for a year and got to live on the island for free with a salary of $100,000. A number of baby-product sites run cute baby photo contests. Incorporating multi-media into contests is easier than ever before. As a bonus, include user voting as a part of the selection criteria to encourage people to share and activate their social networks.

Strategic Reasons for Sharing

Creating and sharing your own content can be an extremely effective social media strategy. We covered strategic reasons for social media marketing in Chapter 2, and sharing can work for any of the strategies, but there are a few that sharing works best with:

- **Humanizing your brand** – Sharing video and photo content of real people from your company or using your product shows the personal side of your business and strengthens relationships. People like to do business with real people.

- **Rewarding customers (building loyalty)** – Sharing success stories of your customers or featuring their testimonials, photos or videos can build loyalty and serve as a way to reward customers.

- **Search engine optimization** – Search engine results include photos, videos and text/website results. By sharing multi-media content related to your business you are increasing the chances that you will show up in search engine results.

- **Generate word-of-mouth** – Having your customers share their stories, photos and videos related to your product increases your overall marketing reach. If a customer uploads a video using your product, chances are that all of their friends will also see that video, driving word-of-mouth.

- **Get traffic to your website** – Sharing content through social news sites (like Digg or Delicious), or through existing social networks like Twitter or Facebook, can drive traffic back to your website. These can be significant sources of traffic to your website and eventually potential customers.

Photo Sharing

Photo sharing is another powerful way to leverage social sharing for marketing. People LOVE to look at photos (especially of themselves or people they know). Photos can be posted online for free where other people can view them and comment on them. In the past few years, with the growth of smartphones that take photos and are connected to the Internet, there has been a huge increase in photosharing on Facebook as well as sites like Instagram.

Many businesses can share photos online as a way to generate awareness or build relationships. A car dealership can share photos of new car owners or of new cars that they have in stock. A hairdresser can take "before" and "after" photos of clients. Restaurants can post photos of their food and drinks. Companies with sales forces can share photos of new (or all) sales reps as a way to build relationships with prospects. Consumer products can share photos of new packaging, or of their product being created, developed or even used. There are clearly lots of different potential venues to share photos.

The most popular photo-sharing site in the world is actually Facebook (which we'll cover in Chapter 9 – Social Networks). Facebook allows users to share photos, but typically (depending on your privacy settings) the photos are only viewable by people in your social network, and not the general public. Instagram is a mobile application that allows users to take photos through their phone and share with their Instagram friends or post on social networks. For businesses that want their photos to be openly available, Flickr (www.flickr.com) is the most popular public photo sharing website. Flickr allows anyone to view photos – even people without accounts on Flickr, whereas Facebook photos may not be open to everyone.

Instagram

Instagram is quickly emerging as a social network to watch in social media. In 2012, Facebook purchased Instagram for $1 billion and the social network now has over 100 million users. Nearly 4 billion photos have been shared on Instagram since its launch, and 40% of brands have already adopted Instagram for marketing.

What is Instagram and How Does it Work?

Instagram is a mobile application that allows users to take and share photos from their mobile phones. Instagram has two primary features. First, it allows users to edit their photos and create beautiful images. Second, it functions as a social network for image sharing.

Similar to most social networks, a user on Instagram can create a profile with basic information, can follow other users, like images and leave comments. Unlike with other social networks, this all takes place through a mobile application and currently cannot be done on the web.

Images from Instagram can easily be shared on Facebook and Twitter, and some users use Instagram primarily as a way to share their photos on other social networks. In addition, Instagram is a social network unto itself. On Instagram, users can view other users' photos (depending on privacy settings) and follow other users, as well as like and comment on images.

How Businesses are Using Instagram

Businesses use Instagram in a variety of ways. At present, there is no difference on Instagram between a personal account and a business account.

Some businesses have corporate accounts on Instagram that they use to take and share images, like Pure Michigan, which is covered in the next section on case studies.

It isn't enough to take photos and hope that your audience will magically build itself. Most of the brands that have been successful in building communities on Instagram spend time interacting with other users by following, commenting and liking photos from other users. Using hashtags (covered in the next section) can also increase your awareness and reach on Instagram.

Instagram can also be a quick and easy way to take photos to share on Facebook, Twitter, or other social networks. If you don't have time to invest in building a community on Instagram, consider using it as a way to create powerful image content.

Similar to Twitter, a hashtag is used as a part of a post to signify the theme of the image and make it searchable. Adding the "#" sign in front of a word or phrase makes it searchable. For example, I may tag a photo with #Cincinnati so that people who search for images of Cincinnati will see my photos.

Brands, businesses and celebrities are taking advantage of using hashtags on Instagram to both theme conversations and to run contests.

For example, Jason Mraz ran a contest asking Instagram users to translate his song "I Won't Give Up" into an image and tag it with #IWONTGIVEUP. A quick search on Instagram shows over 30,000 photos tagged with #IWONTGIVEUP that bring the song to life.

In addition to driving images shared on Instagram the photo contest generated Tweets and Facebook posts from all types of people, including celebrities.

Randy Jackson ✔
@YO_RANDYJACKSON   ✔ Follow

Yo @jason_mraz #iwontgiveup
instagr.am/p/Guq6yWltTA/

8 Feb 12   ← Reply ⟲ Retweet ★
                                              Favorite

Selena Gomez ✔
@selenagomez   ✔ Follow

This is my #iwontgiveup photo. Hana is so beautiful and
one of the most incredible people I've met. Love you
instagr.am/p/GsCcPYRuws/

7 Feb 12   ← Reply ⟲ Retweet ★
                                              Favorite

For example, Brooklyn Bowl created an Instagram contest where customers can share photos tagged with #BrooklynBowl for a chance to win free tickets to a show. To date, over 5,400 photos have been uploaded to Instagram with #BrooklynBowl. One of the key advantages of encouraging Instagrammers to use your hashtag is that you bring your brand into the conversation.

I may be bowling at Brooklyn Bowl and snapping photos of my friends to share on Facebook and Twitter. I would probably include a description of the photo but might not think to mention where the photo was taken. By adding the request to tag my photo with the venue #BrooklynBowl, Brooklyn Bowl is now a part of the discussion and is building awareness for their brand.

Flickr.com

Flickr is a popular photo-sharing site and is owned by Yahoo. Flickr as a site has two main goals: to help people make their photos available to the people who matter to them and to enable new ways of organizing photos and videos.

On Flickr.com, individuals or companies can easily (and for free) upload publically viewable photos. Photos can be tagged, titled and grouped into albums to make the photos easy to find. Essentially, it is an easy want to share photos with the public. Once a photo is uploaded to Flickr it can be shared through Twitter, Facebook or other social networks and also included on a blog or website.

Flickr also allows multiple people to share photos into a single group. A group is free and the creator of the group is able to allow anyone with a Flickr account to also share their photos. For cxample, if you had an event at your business there may be five different people who all have photos from the event. By creating a Flickr group for the event, all of the five people with photos can join the group and contribute their photos to the group photo pool. Then all of the photos from all of the five photographers would be publicly viewable in one place. This makes it easy for people to view photos. In addition, in the settings you can allow (or not allow) people to download photos so that they can get their own copy.

Sharing photos on Flickr has two main advantages over Facebook. First, the images may be indexed by search engines and appear in search engine results. Second, the images can be viewed and used by anyone regardless of whether or not they have an account on Flickr.

Flickr Groups in Action

Here is an example of how Flickr groups can work. One of the conferences that I work with created a photo group for the conference. Let's call it "Conference X 2013." Prior to the conference, the conference marketing coordinator created a Flickr group called Conference X 2013 (which has a unique web address or URL) and told the conference attendees to post their photos in the group. They also told attendees that they could go to the group to view all of the photos from the conference.

At the conference, 50 different people took photos and joined the Conference X photo group on Flickr. They all uploaded their photos and shared them in the Flickr group. The attendees of Conference X could then see all of the photos from the conference in one place and even download and print them if the photographer allows them to. When the attendees see their photos they tell their friends and post them on Facebook and Twitter, which builds even more buzz around the event.

In addition to sharing photos from around your office and creating pools of photos, photo-sharing sites can be used to create and run photo contests. People love to share and post photos online (especially of kids, pets and landscapes). A number of different baby brands have "cute baby contests" where people submit pictures of their baby for a chance to win something. Creating a photo contest can really engage and excite your target audience. The key is to keep the contest relevant to your brand, product or company.

Photo Sharing Example:
Purina PetCentric

People LOVE to show off their pets, and sharing photos is a perfect way for them to show off just how cute their furry friend is. Based on this insight, Purina Petcentric launched a weekly pet photo contest on their Facebook fan page.

To enter the contest, participants simply had to upload a photo to the Flickr group. The Flickr group was free to create and anyone wanting to enter the contest could simply create a free account on Flickr.

Purina chose three finalists each week and the finalists were posted on Facebook where Facebook fans would then vote for the winning photo.

Leveraging Flickr was a simple and free way for Purina to run the photo contest. Once they had some experience with the contest and saw how popular it was, they went on to create a Facebook Petcentric photo contest app so it could be more naturally integrated into Facebook.

Link your photos to other social networks

Similar to video sharing, when sharing photos online through a site like Flickr or Instagram, the photos can also be included on your blog, website, Facebook page, Twitter account, email newsletter or other social profiles. Don't forget to leverage photo-sharing by incorporating your photos in the rest of your online marketing.

Pinterest

Pinterest is quickly emerging as a social media site to watch – it is now the third largest social network and it primarily centers around images. Pinterest is taking the social media world by storm; it is the fastest growing independent social network in the history of social media and it is highly visual. Both individuals and businesses are using Pinterest to share what they love and to build an audience around interesting content.

What is Pinterest and How Does it Work?

Pinterest is your "online pinboard" where "pinners" create boards based on a specific topic and "pin" individual pieces of content related to the board. So I may create a pinboard called "Social Media Infographics" where I share infographics about social media marketing, and another called "Cool Stuff for the Office" where I share the most interesting office accessories, and yet another called "Coffee Addiction" where I share coffee stuff.

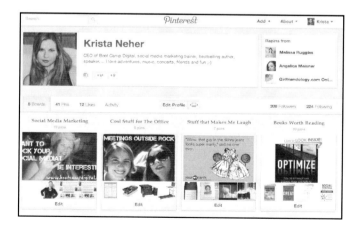

Here are the basics of Pinterest:

- A person or business can have a Pinterest account. There are specific business accounts that you can use to verify that you are a business, but they work the same as a personal account (at this point).

- A "pin" is an individual item or piece of content that is pinned or shared on Pinterest.

- A pinboard is a collection of pins, typically based around a specific topic.

- A Pinterest account or user can have an unlimited number of pinboards with an unlimited number of items pinned within each board.

- When a user logs in to Pinterest, he or she sees a newsfeed (similar to Facebook or LinkedIn) that shows recent pins from pinners that he or she follows.

- Pinterest is a social network – users can follow other people or just specific boards from other people. They can also like, repin and comment on pins posted by others.

- Pins are public, which means that you can search Pinterest to find things that interest you, and even people who don't follow you can find your pins.

- If you want a couple of private boards as well, there are now Secret Boards that only you and those you give permission to can see.

In the example below you can see my friend Lat's Pinterest account. She has a number of pin boards to represent the things that she finds interesting. When she finds a great recipe that she might want to make some day, she pins it to her Yummies board.

It serves as a place for her to share and keep track of the things she is interested in.

Any website or image can be *pinned* on Pinterest, but the way pins are displayed, the images is the primary focus. In the example below we *pinned* a blog post from our website, and the pin shows some desciptive text that we provided as well as the image. If the image isn't descriptive of the con-

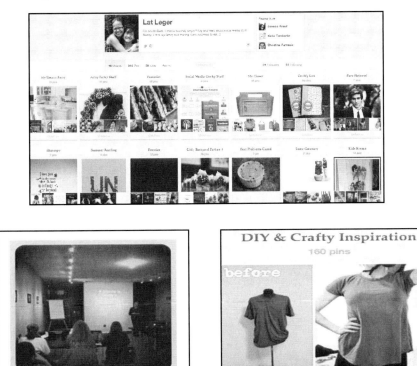

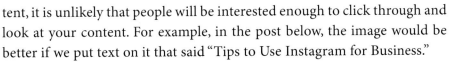

tent, it is unlikely that people will be interested enough to click through and look at your content. For example, in the post below, the image would be better if we put text on it that said "Tips to Use Instagram for Business."

In addition to the pin itself focusing around the image, the board, which is what people will see when they go to your Pinterest account, is centered around your images.

Why Pinterest is Important for Businesses

Pinterest is important for a number of reasons. First, Pinterest is a large social network that is growing quickly. Second, it has highly engaged users.

- Pinterest buyers spend more money, more often than any of the other top 5 social media sites.

- American consumers who use Pinterest follow an average of 9.3 retail companies on the network.

- The number of daily Pinterest users has increased by 145% since January 2012.

One of the main reasons that Pinterest is so powerful for businesses is that it sends massive amounts of traffic to other websites on the internet. Pinterest currently sends more traffic to other businesses than Google+, YouTube and LinkedIn combined. When content is pinned or posted to Pinterest, people often click on it to find the original source of the pin, which sends the user to the website where the content is hosted. Pinterest is the #1 source of traffic to MarthaStewart.com.

For example, I might find a great pair of shoes pinned to Pinterest and want to see where they are for sale. I can click on the shoes and go to Amazon.com (or whatever site the shoes were originally from) and purchase them. Alternately, I might find a great home décor idea, and I want to see exactly how the room was put together and find more details, so I'll click on the image and go to the page on MarthaStewart.com with the article and image.

Pinterest is a highly "viral" social network, which means that content on Pinterest can spread quickly. 80% of pins on Pinterest are repins, which means that Pinners like to share content that is already on the site. This means that sharing your content on Pinterest could mean that it gains views and repins quickly.

Pinterest is also great for businesses because it is public. You can search for pins, boards or users on almost any topic to see what people are pinning. On Pinterest you can follow anyone (they don't have to approve you like Facebook) and anyone can follow you.

How Businesses are Using Pinterest

Businesses use Pinterest to achieve a number of marketing objectives:

- **Traffic** - To drive traffic to their website by pinning their content (blog posts with images, infographics, product pictures, etc.).

- **Branding** - To bring their brand to life by creating boards that showcase what their brand stands for.

- **Awareness** - To build awareness by getting in front of the audiences they want to connect with.

- **Sales** – To increase direct sales as a result of their participation on Pinterest.

- **Community** – To build community and deepen connections with their audience by engaging and participating on Pinterest.

- **Resource** – To create a resource for press, employees, customers, etc. By creating pinboards with comprehensive information about a given topic, Pinterest can become a visual resource guide.

- **Research** – To understand the content that people share.

Slide Show Presentation Sharing

Slide show sharing is a relatively new category of sharing, but it can be very effective. Using sites like Slideshare.net, you can share PowerPoint presentations. If you are creating PowerPoint presentations, you can easily upload them to www.slideshare.net for free. Slideshare will make your presentation publicly viewable and you can even allow people to download it.

If you give presentations on subject areas that your target audience is interested in, sharing them on Slideshare is a no-brainer. If the slide show is already created it only takes a few extra minutes to upload and share the presentation on Slideshare. Sharing a presentation on Slideshare can be a great way to build general awareness and position yourself or your company as an expert.

In addition, if you are an industry speaker, posting your presentations on Slideshare is an easy way to make your presentation available to conference attendees.

Slide Show Sharing Example:

Krista Neher

Every year I am asked to speak at a variety of industry conferences, keynotes, trade shows and colleges. I create

PowerPoint presentations for these speeches, and I am often asked where people can find them after the presentation.

In 2009, I created an account (for free) on Slideshare and started uploading some of my presentations. In 2009, I uploaded 11 slideshows. I probably only spent about an hour in total (since I had already created the content). Over the year my 11 presentations received almost 10,000 views and were featured on the homepage of Slideshare twice. That means that nearly 10,000 people were exposed to my brand and ideas. In 2013 Slideshare is even more effective with many of my presentations generating over 1,000 views each.

In addition, some of my speaking opportunities came directly from people who had seen my presentation on Slideshare and wanted me to do a similar presentation for their group. Slideshare resulted in brand awareness and real business for me.

Similar to other sharing platforms, Slideshare presentations can be incorporated into websites, blogs, Facebook or linked to in Twitter. Get the most out of your Slideshare presentation by sharing it on your other social networks and online marketing sites.

A word of caution when using sites like Slideshare: be aware of how much of your content you want to share for free – especially if it is your intellectual property. When I started using Slideshare I allowed people to download my presentation. I realized that people who were downloading my presentation were probably reusing my slides without my permission. Many Internet users are not aware of copyright laws. I immediately changed my setting on Slideshare and I am now careful about how much intellectual property I post online.

PDF File Sharing

PDF file sharing is also a newer form of social media sharing. Similar to slide show sharing, to share a PDF on a site like Scribd.com you simply create a free account and upload your PDF file. Slideshare.net also now offers PDF sharing in addition to slide show presentation sharing.

PDF file sharing is a great way to share documents that you don't want others to be able to copy or edit. PDF sharing can work for white papers (if you won't require an email address to receive the white paper) or sales sheets.

The advantage of sharing PDF documents on Scribd is that the content of the document can be indexed by search engines, and people can view your content without having to download a file.

Similar to other sharing tools, PDF files shared on Scribd.com can be posted across other social networks and websites to increase the viral sharing of your content.

Social News and News Sharing Sites

In the age of social media, everything can be social – including news. According to Wikipedia[46]:

> The term **social news** refers to websites where users submit and vote on news stories or other links, thus determining which links are presented.
>
> Social news was pioneered by community sites like Slashdot and Fark. It became more popular with the advent of Digg, which combined Delicious and Slashdot's features. Digg and Delicious have a number of other competitors in the social news business, with one of their biggest being Reddit.
>
> More recently, the social news phenomenon has spawned a number of news aggregator niche sites such as Sphinn (internet marketing), Techmeme (tech news), Socialnews.biz (business news) and Sphere (top news). These collect and group articles based on growing web interest—presenting users with a reflexive news feed.

There are hundreds of social news sites that range from general news sites to niche specific sites. Essentially, a social news site is a site where the news that rises to the top is based on user voting and popularity. Social news sites leverage *the Wisdom of Crowds* in that the masses decide which news is most relevant. Users are given the editorial power to influence the visibility of content. The news that rises to the top is determined by an algorithm or formula that varies between different social news sites. Most social news algorithms include a number of factors like number of votes, popularity and influence of voters, number of comments, etc.

Social news sites are popular because they help people discover interesting news they might normally miss but also because the sites or news stories that rise to the top get huge spikes in traffic. Many bloggers try to get their blog posts to the top of social news sites as a way to increase traffic and readers.

Social news sites are popular with bloggers and marketers because they are an excellent way to disseminate ideas and attract traffic and attention. Marketers can use social news sites to share news that is relevant to their industry as a way of building credibility in their industry. Constantly sharing interesting new stories can position you as an expert on your subject area. Posting on social news sites provides you with a platform to showcase your ideas to a larger audience than the people who are regularly reading your content.

Again, if you have a publishing strategy where you are creating content, you should consider using social news sites to generate traffic and an audience for your content. This allows you to increase your visibility and the traffic to your website.

Social Bookmarking

Social news sites focus on sharing specific news articles and posts whereas social bookmarking focuses on sharing web pages (which may be articles, blog posts, websites or any webpage). According to Wikipedia[47]:

> **Social bookmarking** is a method for Internet users to share, organize, search, and manage bookmarks of web resources. Unlike file sharing, the resources themselves aren't shared, merely bookmarks that reference them.
>
> In a social bookmarking system, users save links to web pages that they want to remember and/or share. These bookmarks are usually public, and can be saved privately,

---

47 http://en.wikipedia.org/wiki/Social_bookmarking

shared only with specified people or groups, shared only inside certain networks, or another combination of public and private domains. The allowed people can usually view these bookmarks chronologically, by category or tags, or via a search engine.

Social bookmarking sites often highlight or showcase bookmarked webpages that are the most popular, as determined by a number of factors. Popular social bookmarking sites include Delicious (www.delicious.com) and StumbleUpon (www.stumbleupon.com). StumbleUpon is also a social bookmarking recommendation system, where you can see what your friends are bookmarking and popular sites. StumbleUpon lets you "Discover cool stuff personalized to you" by showing bookmarks that you might like based on your interests, friends and people like you.

People who use social bookmarking sites typically use them to find interesting and relevant website and webpages. Marketers like social bookmarking sites because similar to social news sites, they provide the opportunity to syndicate and disseminate content that increases exposure of your content and brings a new audience to your site. If you are publishing content, social bookmarking sites can be a major traffic driver to your site.

Additionally, similar to social news sites, just participating has benefits. By sharing relevant and insightful pages, you can become a sought after resource and influencer.

Music Sharing

Music sharing is a way that people can share music online. Music sharing sites allow you to select songs that you like and create customized playlists or stations. Your friends can then go to your music sharing site profile and listen to the music that you are currently sharing.

Music sharing sites typically do not allow users to actually download the music file, they simply allow the file to be played from a particular website. Popular music sharing sites like Blip.fm (www.Blip.fm), Spotify (www.spotify.com) and Pandora (www.pandora.com) livestream music from the web and allow users to like and share their musical tastes with their friends.

The business uses for music are probably quite limited unless your business is in the music or entertainment industry. If you are in these industries, it might be worth considering creating a profile on a music-sharing site to keep your fans up to date on the music that you are listening to. The music from these sites can also be embedded in your websites, blogs and social profiles to share with others.

On-Site Sharing Tools

There are a number of sharing buttons or "widgets" you can add to your website, blog or podcast to make it easy and encourage people to share your content. A sharing tool/plugin/widget is a button that appears on a webpage that makes sharing easier by directly connecting with other sharing tools like email, Twitter, social news sites, etc.

One button you can add is the "ShareThis" button. Including this on a web page allows you to choose from a variety of options (email, Facebook, Twitter) and immediately share the website on that social network. For example, if I clicked on the "Email" button my email would automatically open with an email ready to send with a link to the article. If I click the "Facebook" button, my Facebook account will automatically open with the article link and title ready to post.

If you are writing a blog or have a website, using something like the "ShareThis" button (found at www.Sharethis.com), makes it easy and encourages people to share your content. Studies from ShareThis actually show that including the button on your webpage results in more people sharing your content.

Including a sharing button on your website is a simple way to increase the number of people who will share your content with their social network and ultimately increase traffic to your site.

RSS – Really Simple Syndication

RSS stands for Really Simple Syndication and is a way to get updates when content changes on a website. An RSS Feed is a feed that will provide you with updates when content is added to a website. RSS feeds are typically used to stay up to date on new blog posts, news articles or podcasts. According to Wikipedia[48]:

An RSS document (which is called a "feed", "web feed", or "channel") includes full or summarized text, plus metadata such as publishing dates and authorship. Web feeds benefit publishers by letting them syndicate content automatically. They benefit readers who want to subscribe to timely updates from favored websites or to aggregate feeds from many sites into one place.

RSS feeds can be read using software called an "RSS reader", "feed reader", or "aggregator", which can be web-based, desktop-based, or mobile-device-based. The user subscribes to a feed by clicking an RSS icon (shown below) in a web browser that initiates the subscription process. The RSS reader checks the user's subscribed feeds regularly for new work, downloads any updates that it finds, and provides a user interface to monitor and read the feeds.

Think of an RSS feed as the difference between getting a newspaper or magazine subscription and going to the newsstand. If you have a subscription every new issue is delivered right to your door when it comes out – you don't have to make a separate trip to the newsstand.

Let's translate this to the web. If you read 10 different blogs it can be very time-consuming to remember to check each blog and see what is new. Instead of checking each blog, you can *subscribe* to the *RSS Feed* and you will see all of the new articles summarized in the inbox of your newsreader. This makes it easier and more efficient to stay up-to-date on the blogs or websites you read.

A Note on Copyright

When sharing content on the web, it is important to consider copyright requirements, both for the content that you create and for the content you use.

When sharing content like videos, photos, slideshows or documents, be sure to clearly state whether or not the work is copyrighted, and what the copyright or license includes. If your work is your intellectual property and you do not want others to use it, be sure to look at the copyright and usage guidelines for the site that you are sharing on. Also, be sure to mark

---

48 http://en.wikipedia.org/wiki/RSS

your work as copyright protected. Most sites that allow you to share content will allow you to determine if you want others to be able to download your content, reuse your content or share your content on their own sites. Be sure to clearly communicate how your content can be used.

When you are creating content, you also need to think about copyrighted work that may be integrated in your content. Since the work is being created for commercial usage, the laws are fairly strict on what you can and can't use. Consult with your lawyer prior to sharing content that may include the copyrighted work of others. For example, when creating a video, you need to have a license to use music. In photos, you may need model releases of the people being photographed, and you need to be cautious about including the trademarked works of other brands (like their logos). Be sure to consult with a lawyer when sharing content to understand the complexities of copyright and legal issues.

ACTION ITEMS AND KEY LEARNINGS

Want to put the Social Media Field Guide into Action?
Go to www.bootcampdigital.com/actionplanner to
download your FREE Field Guide action planner.

CHAPTER 9:

Social Networks

- - - - - - - - - - - - - - - -

Social networks are one of the most popular areas of social media marketing, and Facebook and LinkedIn are the two largest social media sites online. In addition, marketers, recruiters, sales professionals, human resources and business development departments are all leveraging social networks to build connections. The main social networks are Facebook, LinkedIn, Google+ and MySpace. MySpace has been declining dramatically over the past few years and is now only relevant for a few niche marketing purposes, so it will not be discussed in detail in this section.

Social Networks
LinkedIn

LinkedIn is a growing social network with a more affluent, business-oriented audience. LinkedIn is primarily a business networking social network – it is where business professionals post their online resumes and connect with other business professionals. The opportunities for marketers on LinkedIn are more limited than on Facebook – there aren't as many ways for companies to communicate en masse with users. LinkedIn works well for B-to-B marketing, business development, sales, recruiting or individuals looking to promote their personal brand and build their reputation.

LinkedIn is a very powerful but underutilized social network. LinkedIn allows businesses and individuals to gain industry prominence by connecting with other industry professionals based on shared interests. Similar to real world networking events, on LinkedIn you can meet other professionals via relevant groups, and gain prominence in your industry by positioning yourself or your company as a thought leader.

How LinkedIn Works

LinkedIn is a site primarily aimed at helping business professionals connect with people they know and leverage the networks of people they know. To join LinkedIn, simply create a free account and profile. A LinkedIn profile typically consists of basic resume information as well as a profile headline and business interests. **Be sure to fully complete your LinkedIn profile to get the best results and put your best foot forward.** Your LinkedIn profile is essentially an online resume.

In addition to creating a profile, LinkedIn can be used to connect with business contacts. Adding contacts to LinkedIn helps you stay up-to-date with your contacts and what they are doing. In addition, by posting your information on LinkedIn, your contacts can stay up-to-date with you. Similar to real-life networking, staying top-of-mind with business contacts drives results over time.

In addition to adding your own contacts, LinkedIn can be used to expand your business network. Once you are active on LinkedIn, you can start to see who your connections are connected to. So, if you wanted to connect with John Smith (perhaps he is a sales prospect, works for a company you are interested in, etc.), you can see who else in your network is connected to him and request an introduction. This allows you to grow and expand your network.

A word of caution about adding connections on LinkedIn: LinkedIn is *very strict* in respect to network building – if too many of your requests to connect with people are denied or ignored (i.e., the person doesn't know you), you will be banned from adding new people or have your profile deleted. When connecting on LinkedIn, be sure to connect with people you know, or provide context around why you are making new connections so that your requests are not denied.

LINKEDIN MARKETING OPPORTUNITY:
Searching for People

One of the most valuable tools in LinkedIn is the search capability. LinkedIn allows you to search for people based on a variety of factors – company, job title, name, location, professional status, etc. Once you find a person, you can also see if they are connected to any of your contacts.

LinkedIn search is very valuable for sales, business development and recruiters. For example, a company that I worked with was looking to present their new product to digital strategists at advertising agencies. The challenge was finding out who the digital strategists were in order to initiate a phone conversation. Through LinkedIn, we were able to search for digital strategists at specific advertising agencies. We then called the switchboard of the advertising agency and requested by name the exact person we needed to connect with. This made the sales process much simpler.

LinkedIn can also be used to move you even closer to building relationships vs. cold calling. A friend of mine wanted to do a deal with a major television network, but he wasn't sure how to begin and connect with people. We went on LinkedIn and found that a friend of his was also connected to a VP at the network that he was trying to reach. He messaged the friend and requested an introduction to the VP. The friend then emailed the VP and made a friendly introduction and a deal was closed within a month. Rather than cold calling or searching for people randomly, building your LinkedIn connections and looking at who they are connected to can drive business results quickly.

A final example of the power of LinkedIn search is in recruiting. LinkedIn allows you to search for keywords in profiles and geography. You can use this to find and connect with potential candidates, and to screen them prior to reaching out. I typically get a few emails a week from recruiters looking for social media professionals. They search for social media marketing professionals and send emails to qualified people encouraging them to apply. Even though I'm not interested, I am usually able to recommend a few of my connections for them.

LINKEDIN MARKETING OPPORTUNITY:
Groups

LinkedIn groups can increase your visibility and lead to new business opportunities. Just like real-life networking groups, LinkedIn groups can have the same benefits of increasing your network and visibility. There are LinkedIn groups for almost any subject area and you can search for groups on LinkedIn that are relevant to your business area. There are groups for doctors, lawyers, real estate agents, furniture associations, etc. If you can't find a group appropriate to your business area, you can create a new one.

To take advantage of LinkedIn groups:

- **Join** groups related to your industry or where your target audience is. Joining a group and allowing members to contact you can lead to new opportunities.

- **Discuss** topics on the discussion page. Discussions are valuable because they are displayed first on the group page and in notification emails to users. Respond to discussion posts from people you want to connect with (it is a great way to build a relationship) or start your own discussion. You can also post your blog as a discussion item.

- **Post** news items into relevant groups to gain visibility. You can also use news posts to promote your blog. News also now has voting so you can vote up articles that you like.

- **Jobs** can be posted into groups.

- **Subgroups** can be created to provide even more specificity in a group. Joining subgroups can help you get even more specific with your target audience.

- **Creating a group** can also be extremely valuable. As the group creator you have the opportunity to connect with everyone who joins your group and you are seen as a leader and connecter in the industry. This not only expands your network, but also allows you to message the entire group.

LINKEDIN MARKETING OPPORTUNITY:
Staying Active and Top of Mind

The key to success in LinkedIn Marketing is to stay active and top-of-mind. When I train businesses on social media marketing, I use a proven success system that provides an exact method for businesses to strategically leverage LinkedIn with less than twenty minutes, a few times a week. Joining LinkedIn isn't enough – you need to stay active to derive real business value. Continuous activity improves your visibility, which can lead to opportunities.

Reasons to stay active on LinkedIn:

- You show up in LinkedIn activity reports that are emailed out to your connections – which keeps you top-of-mind with your network

- You show up on the profiles of those you interact with – which increases your reach

- Your name is included in group emails – which increases your visibility within the group

Activities to Stay Active on LinkedIn:

- Update your status

- Post to a group

- Add connections

- Update your profile

- Recommend a co-worker

- Request recommendations

The larger your network and the more visible you are, the more likely you are to gain opportunities from LinkedIn.

LINKEDIN MARKETING OPPORTUNITY:
Business Pages

Most of the marketing activities discussed above involve individual profiles on LinkedIn. Participation in groups or connecting with people through LinkedIn search is done at an individual level through a personal profile.

The only place for a business entity to create a presence on LinkedIn is through a business page. A business page allows the business to provide some basic information, upload an image, post status updates, highlight their products or services and even request recommendations.

It is helpful for any business to have a LinkedIn business page, and it doesn't take long to setup. Business pages often show up at the top of Google search results for a business so they are an excellent opportunity to extend your brand footprint online. Additionally, if you hire regularly, LinkedIn can be very valuable to connect with prospects.

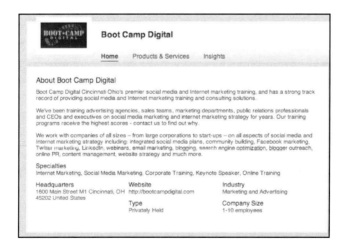

However, when looking at traffic generated to LinkedIn business pages, it is typically fairly limited, with the exception of large organizations. Page analytics allows you to see how many people are viewing your page each week. Look at the amount of traffic that your page receives to determine the amount of effort that you will put into it. For example, Boot Camp Digital receives only one view a day, which is significantly less than other social networks. So, we created a strong branded presence on our page to be sure that we look good when people find it, but we don't prioritize it as a social network to continuously update.

Social Networks:
Facebook

Facebook is the largest and fastest growing social network in the US, and it has over a billion users globally. Facebook allows you to connect with people you know; share your profile; post photos; share news and links; update your status; participate in groups; play games; become a fan of people, brands or products; and much, much more.

Facebook is a place for people to connect with friends, family and other people they know. Unlike LinkedIn where you can search for people based on their company or keywords contained in their profile, Facebook does not allow broad searching – you need to know whom you are trying to connect with or be a member of a group or network.

Facebook also has a number of opportunities for businesses to connect with people. Eighty percent of Facebookers are connected with brands and businesses on Facebook and an average Facebook user is connected to 80 pages, events and groups.

Prior to investing in creating Facebook assets, ask yourself what your marketing goals are and what you will give the members of your group/event/page that is of value. Many people sign up for a group or page never to return. You have to do more than create a page – engage your users.

How Facebook Works

Facebook is a social network for connecting with friends and family and sharing status updates, photos or videos. In addition, Facebook allows users to "like" pages of celebrities, brands and businesses; post and join events; or join groups based on shared interests.

Individuals typically join Facebook to share what they are doing and to stay up to date with their friends. For example, I can see pictures of my best friend Linda's new daughter when she posts them on Facebook, even though she lives in Texas and we don't talk on the phone every day. I can also look at her status updates where she posts information about how things are going. I can leave comments on the photos or status updates to create a two-way conversation. Facebook is a great way to stay up-to-date and interact with family and friends.

In addition to personal use of Facebook, there are also many opportunities for businesses to participate. Businesses can create *pages,* which are the official presence of a business on Facebook. Fans and friends can then publicly "like" the fan page to show their connection with your business and stay up to date. Businesses can also leverage groups, events and ads. As shown in the graph below from a Morpace study, people talk about brands on Facebook and are influenced by referrals from Facebook friends.

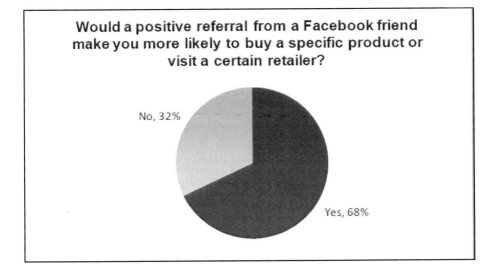

FACEBOOK MARKETING OPPORTUNITY:
Pages

Facebook states that *"only the official representative of an artist, business, or brand may create a Facebook Page."* Pages are intended to be an "official" web page for your organization on Facebook. This is where most businesses start on Facebook – creating a fan page. Once the fan page is created people can "like" the page, which means that it will publicly display in their profile and they will see your status updates and posts in their newsfeed.

Facebook fan pages allow businesses to stay connected with their fans by sharing information. Once a business has a fan page they can post status updates, which appear on their Timeline and are also displayed in the newsfeed of their fans.

According to a study[49], people connect with brands on Facebook for a variety of reasons. The most popular reason is to let their friends know about the businesses, brands and products that they support. In addition, people like pages to get deals and discounts and to learn about new products. It is easy to see how this can lead to marketing value. Creating a great fan page requires strategic thinking and a solid content plan. A number of businesses that we have worked with have seen results by using our fan page methods outlined in the Boot Camp Digital Training Programs.

49 http://www.morpace.com/Omnibus-Reports/Omnibus%20Report-Facebooks%20Impact%20on%20Retailers.pdf

The primary challenge that most businesses face on Facebook is generating visibility. While a business may create a page, the first step is to acquire fans or "likes" of the page. Once a Facebook user has liked a business page, they may begin to see the udpates from the page in their newsfeed when they log on to Facebook.

Facebook uses an algoythm or math to decide how posts are displayed in a newsfeed. When a user logs on to Facebook, their newsfeed shows them what their friends, pages, events and groups have posted recently. The news that is shown isn't the most recent, it is what Facebook believes is most relevant to the person.

The content posted by business pages on Facebook often doesn't make the cut of being relevant enough to make it into the top of the newsfeed. This means that many of your fans or people who have liked your page will not see your posts. Estimates say that only 7% - 17% of the people who liked your page will actually see your content.

So how do you break through, or is it just a waste of time?

Don't write off Facebook just yet. What this means is that GOOD content is more likely to be seem by more people. Spend time optimizing your content to be sure that you are posting content that people "like" and interact with (comment, click on, share). By posting content that people interact with, your page posts are more likely to receive priority on the Facebook newsfeed of your fans.

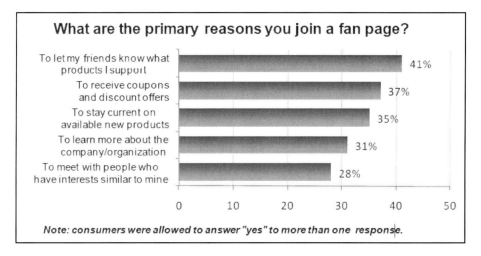

Facebook also allows businesses to pay to promote their posts, or run advertisements to acquire new fans. Facebook ads can be a good way to reach your target audience and promote your page.

As the Social Media Field Guide demonstrates, the key to a strong social marketing strategy is content, which is why it is in the center of the compass.

FACEBOOK MARKETING OPPORTUNITY:
Groups

Facebook groups can be created by anyone to promote interests, causes or anything of interest. A group is something that people join based on a shared interest. Groups are a great marketing opportunity because typically, more people will join a group based on a shared interest than a fan page. In addition, a group allows you to reach people who haven't already heard about your business.

Facebook groups exist around a variety of subject areas and you can join a group or create your own. When I ran marketing for the photography company we found and participated in a number of Facebook photography groups. This helped us to keep a pulse on the photography community and allowed us to generate awareness for our new website. The key was that we didn't overtly post self-promotional messages on the group. We participated in a way that was authentic and built real relationships with photographers.

If there isn't already a group that is relevant to your business, you can create one. One of my coaching clients has a real estate business and was looking to reach first time homebuyers. They created a group called First Time Home Buyers in CityY and got hundreds of group members in only a few days. The group generated more participation than their fan page. This gives them a direct line into their target market.

Another client had a product in targeting students entering post-graduate programs as well as the admissions office. I suggested that in addition to the fan page, we create a group that could be a resource. People are more likely to join a group based on a shared interest than they are to become a fan of a particular company – especially one that they haven't heard of yet. We created a group based on subjects that his audience would be interested in as a way of creating a community where they can connect and share information. In only a few weeks he had a thousand members in his group – and they were people who were in his target audience. The fan page, on the other hand, only had a few hundred members, most of whom were his friends and family. By using groups, he was able to extend his reach and connect with people in his target audience.

FACEBOOK MARKETING OPPORTUNITY:
Events

If your organization is hosting an event, Facebook is a great way to gain visibility and communicate with those interested in attending. An event can easily be created for free by anyone on Facebook.

Creating an event in Facebook provides visibility for the event – each time an attendee says they are attending, the event shows up in their news feed. This can create viral spread for your event.

For example, in my news feed I saw that a friend of mine was attending a networking happy hour the next week. I clicked on the event and decided that I would go too. By posting on Facebook, your events can have more spread. Events can also spread the "invite a friend" option. By encouraging your attendees to invite their Facebook friends, the event can become even more visible.

In addition to the viral spread, Facebook events allow you to keep attendees and invitees up to date. Event creators can send updates and reminders and post information on the event page. Many retailers and restaurants have the opportunity to better leverage Facebook events for their sales or special events.

Building Your Business with Facebook

Facebook gets a lot of hype because it is a large, high growth site. The reality is that many marketers fail to see benefits from their Facebook efforts because they have no clear idea how to leverage their pages. They hire social media consultants or ask a friend to help them create a page, but they have no clear plan of what to do with it and no *content* plan.

The key to success here is sharing content that your target audience is interested in – does this sound familiar yet?

Optimize your content for Facebook by creating short and interesting updates and sharing photos. Look at popular pages in your category to view the content that people on Facebook are most likely to click on and interact with.

Build a creative content plan that posts highly relevant and interesting content that actually engages your fans vs. boring updates.

Social Networks:
Google+

Google launched their social network Google+ in June of 2011 and it was the fastest growing social network ever, adding over 30 million users in the first month, despite being invitation only. Google+ now boasts over 250 million users, but Google+ users are not very active on the site.

For perspective, an average user spends 7.5 hours a month on Facebook, 98 minutes a month on Pinterest and only 3.3 minutes a month on Google+. While Google+ may have a lot of registered users, they aren't spending any time on the site.

What Is Google+ and How Does It Work?

Google+ is Google's social network, and it operates similarly to Facebook. Users can connect with friends and share status updates, photos and videos. Google+ has some additional functionality that allows users to do group video chats (called Hangouts) and also has different ways of organizing contacts (into Circles).

Anyone can create a Google+ profile and add friends to their circles and share status updates. It is free and easy to create an account.

The reality is that while many people have Google+ accounts, very few people are actually using Google+ to share updates and connect with friends. Google+ does not have many people actively using it.

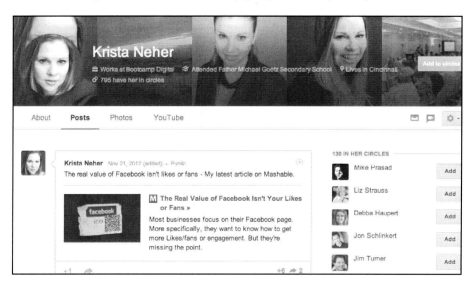

Opportunity for Businesses

Google+ represents the opportunity for businesses to participate with a business page (similar to Facebook). Like Facebook, a business page must be created by an individual with a profile. Business pages currently don't have a lot of functionality – they are mostly limited to updating statuses and sharing photos and videos. They do not currently have the robust features and applications that Facebook pages do.

Most business pages on Google+ have a relatively small number of people following their page. Even the largest brands have a fraction of the fan base that they have on Facebook and the fans are less engaged. Since most Google+ users don't log on regularly, they don't see posts from pages very often so there are fewer engagements with page posts.

It is definitely worth creating a business page for your organization – even if you don't have the capacity to update it regularly. Since Google also controls search, and most businesses want to increase visibility with search engines, it is important to have a Google+ page for your business. Even posts on Google+ are starting to show up on search engines, so posting to your Google+ page is a good strategy for search engines if not as a social media strategy.

As Google continues to place emphasis on Google+ and combines more Google features with Google+ pages and profiles, building and growing a presence on Google+ will become more important.

The bottom line is that Google+ is a site to watch, and getting started early can give you a competitive advantage.

Creating Your Own Social Network

Many people's biggest nightmare is throwing a party and nobody showing up. This is a BIG risk in launching your own social network. What if you launch the network or discussion forum and nobody shows up? What if people aren't interested in creating a community around your brand? What if they don't have anything to talk to each other about? These are real concerns when creating a social network on your own site.

People are already members of a number of social networks and are hesitant to join yet *another*. That being said, if you can create a compelling reason with a focused subject area, you can run a successful branded community.

Creating a community on your own site is easier than ever before. You can use software like Ning.com where you can create a community for free and then upgrade to a paid account where you can customize the content. Businesses can also use different software programs that plug-in directly to your site to create your own customized community on your website.

There are a few key questions to ask before launching your own community:

- **Do you have a big enough audience?** Is your audience big enough to warrant a community? You typically want to have a few thousand people as a minimum to create an active and engaged community.

- **Is your audience engaged?** Even if you have a lot of people on your site, they may not be actively engaged or interested enough in your subject area to create a community. Are they already leaving multiple comments on your blog? Do they show signs of wanting to connect with each other? Look for signs of interest in active engagement and connections before launching your own community.

- **Is your subject area conversational?** The point of a community is for people who share a common interest to connect with each other. Not all subjects are conversational. Look for subject areas that people are naturally interested in talking about to build in to your community.

- **What is your niche?** There are already LOTS of social networks out there. For people to join yours and create *another* user name, password and profile you have to offer them connections around a niche that they can't find anywhere else. Look for a specific subject area, problem, interest or passion point to launch your community around.

- **Who will moderate?** Most communities involve creating profiles and participating in discussions or sharing content. There is always the risk of people sharing inappropriate content or trying to overtly market and post spam in your community. For these reasons it is important to have a moderator who can look at the content and determine whether or not it is appropriate.

- **Who are my 1%, 9% and 90%?** It is said that online, 1% of people are regular participants, 9% are infrequent participants and 90% will view and never participate. This means that for every 100 people in your community, only 1 (on average) will participate regularly, 9 may contribute content when they feel strongly and 90 will browse and never actively participate. It is important to know if you have enough of the 1% and 9% who are interested in participating to create a vibrant community and provide content for the 90% to read.

- **Open or closed?** An on-site community can be open to everyone or restricted to members only. Depending on your marketing goals and objectives with the social network, you'll have to decide if the network should be open or closed. Creating an open network where anyone can see the content can provide search engine benefits and may increase your reach as people find the community content valuable. At the same time, a closed community gives you more control and allows you to provide exclusive content to members.

Can existing social networks meet your needs?

There are already *lots* of social networks out there that have mass adoption like Facebook, Google+ and LinkedIn. Rather than creating your own social network, can you create a group on an existing social network?

Using an existing social network can increase your participation rate since the barriers to join are lower – the users already have an account and it just takes the click of a button. You can also benefit from the regularity with which people log in to their social networks. Over 50% of Facebook users log in every day[16] and Facebook now has almost 50% penetration across all age demographics. Since they are already on the site, it is easy for them to participate in your community – much easier than expecting them to go to your site every day. In addition to reach and frequency, you can gain more visibility due to the viral nature of social networks – if my friends see that I joined your Facebook group they may also join, or I can recommend it to them.

However, there are downsides to building your community on existing social networks. First, you have less control over the setup of the network. Facebook and LinkedIn have limitations on the functionality of groups and fan pages, so you may not be able to create a robust experience. The other issue with using existing social networks is that you are at the mercy of changes to their functionality or terms of service. Social networks like Facebook, Google+ and LinkedIn change the way their features work and what companies are allowed to do on their site pretty regularly. They can delete your group or fan page and they can also remove features that you are using at any time.

It is important to weigh the pros and cons of using existing communities versus building your own. Existing social networks provide a number of benefits but also create risks.

ACTION ITEMS AND KEY LEARNINGS

Want to put the Social Media Field Guide into Action?
Go to www.bootcampdigital.com/actionplanner to
download your FREE Field Guide action planner.

CHAPTER 10:

Microblogging (Twitter)

Twitter has quickly grown to become one of the most popular, yet most misunderstood, social media marketing tools. Twitter has been adopted by celebrities like Oprah and Ashton Kutcher; a variety of different businesses like Home Depot, JetBlue and Whole Foods; and small businesses and average people. While Twitter can be an extremely powerful tool when used correctly, businesses and individuals often have a tough time "getting it."

Twitter now has over 500 million users, and depending on how it is measured it is the third or fourth most popular social network online (tied for the most part with Pinterest).

Twitter can be difficult to use because it isn't as straightforward as other social networks. You join Facebook to connect with friends, LinkedIn for business contacts and Twitter for....? Back in 2007, I had the same problem. I initially didn't get why I would want to be on Twitter. Then, once I had a clear purpose for joining – to connect with other people who were interested in social media marketing – it was like a light bulb went off. I got my company started on Twitter and we were one of the first companies to use Twitter. We got great results from it too. Even when Twitter was new and barely known, it was one of our top sources of referral traffic to our website. When used correctly, Twitter can work wonders and I still generate revenue from Twitter today.

I got my first client for Boot Camp Digital through Twitter. The start-up I worked for had been sold recently, and I was debating between a few job offers, or starting my own business. A brand manager at Procter and Gamble had been following me on Twitter and read my blog. He sent me a note saying that they were looking to do *exactly* what I was talking about on my blog. He saw that I used to work there and thought that it might be a good fit. P&G hired me to consult and train them in their first ever social media project as a direct result of Twitter.

What Is Twitter?

Twitter is a free social networking and micro-blogging service that lets you send and read other users' updates known as tweets. Tweets are text-based posts up to 140 characters in length, which are displayed on the user's profile page and delivered to other users who have subscribed to them (known as followers). Twitter allows you to read and share short updates with people who "follow" you or who you follow.

With Twitter, you can broadcast short messages (limited to 140 characters) to a large audience of people who "follow" you. A tweet can be about anything, from "What do Canada and San Francisco have in common? They are both always colder than I think they'll be!" to "Interesting article from eMarketer: Email is still the most popular distribution method http:// bit.ly." There are no rules or guidelines about what you can or can't tweet. The real question is what will be of interest to your followers.

Why Should I Use Twitter?

There are a few things that make Twitter different from other so-cial networks:

- **You can follow anyone and anyone can follow you** – followers do not have to be "approved" and you can follow anyone you choose. Most social networks, like Google+, Facebook and LinkedIn, require you to approve friends and the relationship has to be mutual (i.e., both parties agree to become friends). Since Twitter is an open network, you can use to it expand your network versus just connecting with people you already know.

- **You can search and find new and interesting people** – with Twitter you can search for people who live in your city, have similar interests or tweet about certain subjects and connect with them. Twitter is intended for open and public sharing – so it is easy to discover new people who share your interests. This is also what makes Twitter so popular with marketers – they can find and connect with people based on interests listed in tweets or profiles.

- **You can promote things** – Twitter allows you to broadcast messages to your followers. You can post links to websites, events, blog posts, articles, etc., through your Twitter account. While most accounts that are heavily promotional won't be successful, it can be a part of your tweets. Creating a Twitter stream that combines self-promotion, promoting others, conversation, humor and information is typically more successful than constant self-promotion (although there are exceptions).

- **People are talking about you already** – Chances are that people are already talking about you, your industry, your customers, etc., on Twitter. You should join in the conversation and become a part of the community and discussions.

- **Bottom line** – Twitter can help you grow your network. This is different from other social network sites. Twitter is a **Broadcasting Tool.**

Who is on Twitter?

Tweeters are different than other social network users in a number of important ways:

- Super-user group
- More interested in many subjects, all news categories and:
    - Restaurants
    - Sports
    - Politics, Religion & Personal Finance

  - ⬦ Pop-culture (music, movies, TV and reading all higher than average)

- More likely to buy books, movies, shoes and cosmetics online

- More entrepreneurial – use Twitter to promote their blog/business/etc

- 31% buy coffee online (average is 21%)

- More likely to work part-time (16% versus 11% average)

- $58k average income

- Average of 28 followers and 32 following them

- Not very loyal – 43% could live without Twitter

Lots of People Don't "Get" Twitter. Don't Be One of Them.

Many people join Twitter and just "don't get it". A study of over 300,000 Twitter accounts by Harvard Business School[50] showed that most of the people who sign up for Twitter post once and never return. It isn't because they don't understand how to physically use Twitter – 80% are followed by at least 1 user versus only 60% on other social networks.

Twitter also has a high rate of quitters versus other social networks[51]. Why is this?

Part of what makes Twitter unique is that it can be used in a variety of ways. Compared to LinkedIn (connect with business contacts) or Facebook (connect with friends), reasons for using Twitter and *what* to tweet about are less obvious. Some people use Twitter to connect with business contacts, others only for family and friends, some to meet new people and others to find an audience for their business. Twitter is extremely flexible; it

---

50 Harvard Business School research, June 1, 2009 http://blogs.harvardbusiness.org/cs/2009/06/new_twitter_research_men_follo.html

51 Nielson Online Primary Research, April 28, 2009 http://blog.nielsen.com/nielsenwire/online_mobile/twitter-quitters-post-roadblock-to-long-term-growth/

can be used in many different ways, but this also makes it less obvious exactly how it should be used.

When Twitter first launched, it asked the question "what are you doing?" Nobody actually cares what you are doing all the time

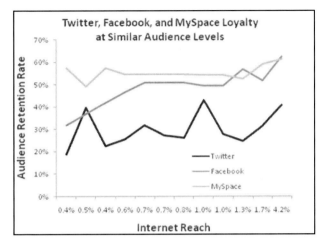

- "getting coffee," "wondering what to eat for dinner." That is the noise of Twitter. Twitter now asks you to share what is interesting, entertaining or remarkable. Tweets might be "Looking for a new coffee shop in the city – anyone have a recommendation? Must have wifi!" or sharing an interesting news article. The key is to tweet things your audience might be interested in.

As a marketer, you can also see the opportunities of connecting with people who tweet these things…. If you owned a coffee house or made coffee, you could respond to the coffee tweet. Remember – Twitter is about sharing what is interesting – not sharing everything.

The real value of Twitter is your ability to expand your network and connect with new people around a common interest, hobby, location, etc. Twitter allows you to expand your network and "meet" new people. By broadcasting messages in a public forum, people can see what you are interested in and connect with you based on shared interests. For example, I did a search for marketing people in Cincinnati and made a number of great connections. When I worked for the photography website, we followed photographers.

How Is Twitter Used?

Twitter is used different ways by different people. You can use Twitter to:
- Update friends and family
- Meet new people in your city
- Meet new people in your industry

- Find people with a hobby or passion
- Find interesting articles
- Stay up to date on news
- Share funny stories
- Share interesting or funny links
- Networking – expand your network
- Personal branding
- Get recommendations
- Get traffic to your blog

How Can Twitter Be Used by Businesses?

Many businesses are now using Twitter. They key to successfully using Twitter to build your business is to remember that you are engaging in social conversations. Overt selling or self-promotion are typically frowned upon by Twitter users. Twitter can add a lot of value, but companies that are successful usually engage in the conversation – they don't just post messages. Companies using Twitter have to add value. Businesses have successfully used Twitter to share:

- Customer service
- Company news
- Find new customers
- Connect with current customers
- Build awareness
- Generate leads
- Provide information
- Discuss subjects that customers are interested in
- Build brand equity
- Get customer feedback
- Run contests
- Offer coupons/free products/sales/deals/discounts
- Get traffic to a blog/website
- Update events
- Provide live coverage of events
- Connect with influencers

- Get media impressions
- Conduct blogger outreach

Twitter Terms

If you are interested in using Twitter for your business, it is important to understand the appropriate etiquette. A number of common Twitter terms appear in the examples below.

Some of the most popular Twitter terms are:

@ The @ symbol is how you publicly reference another Twitter user. For example if you wanted to respond to me or start a conversation you would tweet "@kristaneher – I just read your book. I am really excited about social media now!"

RT RT stands for re-tweet and it is used if you want to re-tweet or forward a tweet to your Twitter stream. For example, if I see a tweet from a friend that I find really interesting and I want to share it with my network, I would re-tweet it.

DM DM stands for direct message and it is a way to send a private message to another person on Twitter.

Commonly known as hashtag or hash-mark, this is a symbol used to reference a popular trend or event. It is a way of tagging tweets around a specific topic area so that people can search for them. For example, when I am at the ad:tech conference I would use #adtech so that people following the conference could search for #adtech and see all of the tweets from the conference.

Marketing Twitter Examples

This book began with the Social Marketing System – strong social marketing starts with listening and understanding the landscape. The next step is to understand your marketing goals and objectives. Since Twitter can be used in so many different ways, having a clear understanding of your marketing objectives is vital to building your Twitter strategy.

Again, it all starts with content, which is at the center of the Social Media Field Guide. Choose your content (what you Tweet about) based on your marketing goals and target audience. When you approach Twitter, it helps to have a clear idea of what you want to achieve.

Build Relationships

- Build relationships with people in your target audience
    - Do a search on keywords related to your product
    - Do a search on your brand and competitors' brands
    - Find # (hashtags) to follow that are relevant
    - Talk back and engage with the community – be funny/interesting

Build Equity

- Build equity for yourself/your brand as caring about people, not just making a sale.
    - Promote others who are relevant
    - Be friendly and kind – just say some nice things to people
    - Offer help/support/kind words for people in your community (beyond just related to your product)

Be an Expert

- Position yourself as an expert in your area – be a thought leader.
    - Tweet interesting articles (they can get retweeted)
    - Tweet your blog posts/webinars – show how you are contributing

- ✧ Engage in intelligent discussions with other thought leaders
- ✧ Provide answers/resources to questions

Drive Sales

- Drive Sales
  - ✧ Host contests
  - ✧ Coupons
  - ✧ Discounts
  - ✧ Sales/promotions
  - ✧ Exclusive Deals

Build Loyalty

- Increase Current Customer Loyalty
  - ✧ Provide online customer service
  - ✧ Respond to brand mentions
  - ✧ Provide something of value to current brand enthusiasts/users

Run Promotions

- Generate sales with promotions
  - ✧ Give special offers on Twitter
  - ✧ Find people searching for your product and offer them a great deal
  - ✧ Promote new product launches
  - ✧ Connect with potential customers

Success on Twitter = Have a Plan

The key to success on Twitter, whether it is for personal or professional use, is to have a clear plan for what you want to do with it (your marketing goals); who you want to connect with (your target audience); and what you are going to talk to them about (your content plan). Sound familiar?

Because Twitter is not as straightforward as other social networks, having a plan is critical. The step-by-step approach of the Social Marketing System will help you achieve results on Twitter.

Before you get started, spend some time listening. Get to know people before tweeting at them. Understand the social norms. Listen to your competitors, the industry and do a few searches. From there, you will be ready to begin developing a Twitter content plan and strategy that will really connect with your audience.

Again, don't be afraid to be flexible. In writing this book, I interviewed Jeff Esposito, the Public Relations Manager at Vista Print. Jeff told me that the PR department started using Twitter as a way to connect with their customers and promote special offers. They quickly found that they were getting a large number of tweets or mentions that were customer service issues. Rather than saying, "Sorry, we don't do customer service on Twitter," they brought their customer service team on-board and created a work process to include them. They are now able to use Twitter to turn around negative mentions of their brand and get real results. As mentioned earlier, in their first year Vista Print sold $25,000 on Twitter.

The key lesson is to be flexible and follow the Social Marketing System through to measure, learn and adapt.

Maximizing Efficiency on Twitter

If you are using Twitter to grow your business online, consider using a tool like Hootsuite (www.Hootsuite.com) to manage your Tweets and schedule in advance. Also, install Twitter onto your mobile phone so you can Tweet on the go.

ACTION ITEMS AND KEY LEARNINGS

CHAPTER 11:

Collaboration and Co-Creation

Collaboration and co-creation are areas that most businesses miss when thinking through their social media marketing plans. Having consumers create with you or leveraging their collective knowledge can be powerful marketing tools. By engaging consumers in the process of creating your product, providing customer service, voting, or sharing their expertise you can build stronger relationships.

What exactly *is* collaboration and co-creation in the context of social media marketing? Collaboration is the opportunity for your customers to collaborate with you, or give their opinion or feedback on something. Co-creation is the ability for customers to actually help you create a product. Both of these tools are great ways to engage customers and generate excitement for your business.

Entire businesses have been built on the notion of the wisdom and power of the masses. Wikipedia, a website that leverages wikis, allows people to contribute to pages of information on almost any subject. It is like an encyclopedia that is created, managed and edited by the general population. Wikipedia uses Wiki technology (we'll discuss that later) that allows anyone to contribute. It sounds like the result of this effort would be a mess of inaccurate data full of rumors, gossip or misinformation. However, a study has shown that Wikipedia is about as accurate as the Encyclopædia Britannica[52]. Additionally, Wikipedia has more entries and is more up to date because new information can be easily included.

That is the power of co-creation.

Leveraging Collaboration for Business

According to Dictionary.com[53], collaboration is:

1. *the act of working with another or others on a joint project*
2. *something created by working jointly with another or others*

Social media is a powerful tool because it allows us to discuss with one another and work together openly, quickly and easily. Social media, therefore, super-charges collaboration because it makes it easy for us to work together on projects both within our social networks and with complete strangers.

Co-creation is slightly different from collaboration, but they are similar. While collaboration emphasizes multiple people working jointly on a project, co-creation is more specific and involves people working together with each other or with a company to create something new. Co-creation can be the creation of a new page on Wikipedia or it can be creating a new product flavor or product features. Co-creation involves leveraging the knowledge of the masses to create something better or new.

Collaboration and co-creation through social media can affect businesses in a variety of different ways:

- **Customer service** – Customer service is expensive and difficult for many companies to maintain. Handling trouble-shooting or problem calls from customers can be a major headache. Collaboration can work well to help customers solve each other's problems. For example, many

---

52 http://news.cnet.com/Study-Wikipedia-as-accurate-as-Britannica/2100-1038_3-5997332.html

53 http://dictionary.reference.com/browse/collaboration

companies have forums where users can ask questions. Questions are answered both by company representatives and other customers. Plus, the question and answer are now publicly available online for others to view. Collaboration can save time and money on customer service.

- **Feedback** – Collaboration is also useful in getting customer feedback or ideas. A simple blog post that asks the question, "Which new feature do you want us to develop first?" can spark huge discussion and help create a new product or feature timeline. Collaboration can lead to customers (or potential customers) sharing their insights with you for free. Listen to the wisdom of your customers and give them a way to share their thoughts on new products, features, technical issues, company policies, etc. This can give you solutions or ideas you may have never thought of.

- **Internal corporate collaboration** – The focus of this book is primarily on leveraging social media for external marketing. However, collaboration can significantly impact your organization internally. If you have multiple employees, leveraging the best knowledge from your work force to solve a problem can be difficult. Tapping into collective knowledge from co-workers can be difficult and in-person meeting may be time-consuming or difficult to arrange. Social technologies like micro-blogging (Twitter), discussion forums, wikis, groups, etc., can help break down barriers and lead to more open and collaborative work environments.

- **New product ideas** – The wisdom of your customers can be used to discuss and improve on new product ideas through collaboration and co-creation. Many brands have run contests or promotions where users can submit new product ideas with the winner receiving a prize. Alternately, these contests can have voting incorporated, where the winner is voted on and the voters help shape and create the new product. New product ideas or features can be a collaborative process (e.g.,. let's discuss together) or through voting (e.g., vote for your favorite flavor).

- **New uses for your product or service** – Leveraging collaboration and co-creation can also create new uses for your product – including ones that you may not have thought of before. Asking customers to submit photos or videos and discuss your product can create eye-opening results. Consider including a contest or prize element for the best idea or the best contributor to the discussions.

- **Marketing contests** – Many brands have used social technologies like YouTube, Facebook, photo sharing, Twitter, blogs and wikis to run co-creation marketing contests. The famous Doritos Super Bowl ad contest had customers create their own ads for Doritos and the winning ad was aired live during the Super Bowl. These contests can create a lot of buzz, allow consumers to really think about your product and show their creativity.

These are only a handful of the potential uses for collaboration and co-creation for businesses. Brands that engage their consumers to help them can create more loyal and passionate fans for their business. People feel a sense of ownership when they have directly participated in the creation of something.

One word of caution when considering collaboration or co-creation: the wisdom of the masses doesn't always work. When looking to engage your customers to help you design or ideate around an idea, it is important to remember that the most popular or most voted-on idea might not always be the best. While there are many instances where the masses work well together (like with Wikipedia), there are many examples of the masses not working well together. Don't let your product ideas fall slave to the lowest common denominator.

Apple, a company that makes industry-changing new consumer electronics products, doesn't look to consumers for too much feedback. Customers have a hard time envisioning something that is dramatically new or different, so they aren't always the best source for new product ideas. Instead, Apple reinvents categories by imagining what is possible, which is something that average consumers are not great at.

Incorporating Collaboration and Co-Creation Tools

A number of tools can facilitate and streamline the process of collaboration and co-creation. Leveraging these technologies will allow you to simply and easily incorporate the wisdom of the crowds into your marketing plan.

Wikis

A wiki is a webpage or website that anyone can edit or change. It is somewhat like a Word document or presentation that is posted on the Internet where anyone can make changes and edit the file at any time. Some wikis have approval processes or filtering applied prior to publishing changes, but the basic premise of a wiki is that it is easy to update. The process of maintaining and updating a wiki is collaborative – many people contribute.

Businesses can create wikis for their products if there is a need to have multiple people to contribute to a document, list or product. For example, when I attended a conference last year, someone at the conference started a wiki that was essentially a list where attendees could share their name and Twitter name. This allowed attendees to connect with each other and know who is attending the conference prior to arriving.

Wikis are great tools when you want multiple people to share information or resources that are available to all.

Of course, with wikis there is the risk of misinformation or malicious posts, so it is important to have a vetting process. With the exception of a few who may try to take advantage of the system, wikis are generally very effective and accurate.

Polls

Polls are simple applications that allow users to select or vote on one or more options. Polls work best when the options are already defined. The best poll questions are specific and simple to answer. They can include things like "Vote for our new flavor" followed by a few options or "What benefit do you most want in your cereal?" The key is to provide a few limited options that people can easily vote on. Be sure to let them know that they are helping to create your future product – their votes matter.

Polls can be run on your own website with simple software, on Facebook, through Twitter with a variety of Tweet Poll services, on your blog with a simple plug-in or on virtually any site you have a presence on. Polls are simple to run and the results are almost instantaneous, making them an easy and affordable co-creation tool for large or small businesses.

Collaborative Feedback Tools

Collaborative feedback tools are emerging as a way for companies to get feedback from customers and share solutions. Popular feedback tools like Get Satisfaction (www.getsatisfaction.com) or User Voice (www.uservoice. com), give consumers a transparent way to give feedback to companies and are typically installed on a website.

The way that collaborative feedback works is that consumers voice their opinion about a company on a specific site – whether it is a complaint or problem, an idea, a question or a compliment. The opinions are publicly posted, creating transparency. Other users can vote for the idea or indicate that they have the same problem. This allows companies to have a clear and transparent view of what their customers are thinking. In addition, customers can share experiences or offer advice. Incorporating tools like these into your website shows that you are open and transparent and gives your customers the opportunity to collaborate with each other.

This is valuable for businesses that can quickly and easily harness the collective wisdom of their customers. Businesses can see which ideas users are more interested in having implemented and follow entire discussions about them. This makes users more engaged in the overall process and can help turn them into brand advocates and enthusiasts.

Discussion Forums

Discussion forums will be discussed in more depth in the next chapter, but discussion platforms essentially allow for a threaded conversation, where a subject can be started or a question can be asked and multiple people can respond to it.

Discussion forums are simple to add to almost any website, or you can use the discussion functionality on other social networks like Facebook or LinkedIn. Discussion forums foster collaboration because the discussion is easy to follow and open to comments.

Social Voting

Social voting is different from polls in that polls ask you to vote for one or more of a number of options. Social voting allows users to "thumbs up" or "thumbs down" an idea to make it rise to the top or sink to the bottom.

For example, social voting can be used to determine the final ideas to be included in a poll.

South by Southwest, a popular technology conference and music/film festival, uses social voting to determine the panels or sessions that will be included at the conference. Ideas are submitted and placed into the Panel Picker, where users can vote up or down ideas and leave comments on the panels. This allows the audience at the conference to choose the subjects that they will listen to. The Panel Picker isn't the only determinant of the panels at the conference. If that was the case, the most popular participants who spend a lot of time getting votes would be the only ones to speak. Instead, user voting and comments accounts for a portion of the process, but an advisory committee makes the final decision.

Marketing Example:
Starbucks "My Idea"

Starbucks launched My Starbucks Idea (http://mystarbucksidea.com/) as a way for consumers to share their ideas back with the company. Consumers can submit ideas or comment on ideas that have been submitted. Starbucks will comment on and acknowledge the ideas, and sometimes even take action.

The Starbucks My Idea site encourages participants to:

> "Share. Vote. Discuss. See.
>
> You know better than anyone else what you want from Starbucks. So tell us. What's your Starbucks Idea? Revolutionary or simple – we want to hear it. Share your ideas, tell us what you think of other people's ideas and join the discussion. We're here, and we're ready to make ideas happen. Let's get started."

The site gets a lot of discussion. When I took another look at the site during the writing of this book, they had six ideas submitted in the previous hour – not bad. Since the launch of the site, they have had over 100,000 product ideas submitted, over 34,000 experience ideas and over 22,000 involvement ideas. They also specifically have a section called "Ideas in

Action" where they highlight the ideas that they have taken action on. Ideas are clearly marked as Under Review, Reviewed, In the Works or Launched.

Some of the launched ideas include donating unsold pastries to local homeless shelters or soup kitchens, selling re-usable sleeves, creating low fat and high protein items for breakfast and building a Starbucks BlackBerry app. What is important about this initiative is that Starbucks isn't just paying lipservice or using this as a tool to streamline complaints. They are taking action and showing a commitment.

Marketing Example:

Create a Hole on Facebook

In preparing for this book, I had the opportunity to interview Dan Schrementi, Director of Gaming Marketing and New Media at Golden Tee. Golden Tee is a golf video game played in bars. Every year, Golden Tee runs a "Create a Hole" contest, in which customers can create and submit their own holes for the game. The winning hole is actually included in the game for next year.

The contest involves users submitting their hole entries. Finalists are selected and the winner is determined by a vote. In the past, Golden Tee ran the voting on their website. This created a number of problems for them since they had to constantly monitor the votes for cheating. It took up a lot of company resources to create and run their own voting system.

A few years ago Golden Tee did something different. Using a Facebook contest application, Golden Tee ran all of the voting for finalists directly through Facebook.

The result?

They saved significant time and resources because the application took care of all of the technical problems with voting. Additionally, in order to vote participants had to become a fan of Golden Tee, so there were able to greatly increase their fan base. The only downside was that there were fewer overall votes cast versus previous years; however, Golden Tee believes that this was more related to eliminating multiple votes as opposed to fewer overall votes. At the end of the promotion, Golden Tee gained fans that they can build relationships with over time and they saved time and money.

ACTION ITEMS AND KEY LEARNINGS

Want to put the Social Media Field Guide into Action?
Go to **www.bootcampdigital.com/actionplanner** to
download your FREE Field Guide action planner.

CHAPTER 12:
Discussion and Review Sites

Discussion and review sites are an extremely important factor in driving purchase decisions online. When you purchase a product from a website, you likely look at how many rating stars it has been given. People who have purchased the product leave a rating and the average rating appears with the product. You may also look at product reviews – what types of experiences have people had with the product?

In addition to on-site ratings and reviews generated by average consumers, a number of "authoritative" sites have "experts" who compare and review products. For example, www.cnet.com is a trusted source for reviews of electronics products. In addition to these review sites, there are also discussion forums that cover a wide variety of topics. Typically on discussion forums, people are asking questions and looking for their peers to help provide solutions.

Discussion forums are a great way to interact with your target audience and answer questions they may have about your product or the category your product is in. For example, if you are selling nutritional supplements, you can respond to questions in discussion forums about the makeup of various supplements, or general nutrition questions.

Discussion Sites

Discussion sites or forums have been around much longer than the term "social media." A discussion forum allows people to start a discussion topic or thread – these will often be discussion areas or questions. Other users can respond to the topic and the conversations are threaded, which means that they appear in order so the conversation can be easily followed.

There are a number of popular discussion sites on the Internet. Yahoo has a very popular site called Yahoo! Answers[54], where questions about a wide variety of topics are asked and other people provide answers. In quickly checking the site, there are questions on a variety of topics and categories ranging from Fantasy Sports, to math, to physics, to drama.

Here are some of the questions posted:

> **Biology help! Please. I dont know what the answer is!!?**
>
> **What Is The Name Of This Song?**
>
> **How do I get Excel to display the contents of the last cell in a row in another location? (what formula?)?**
>
> **Daughter can't get health insurance makes minimum wage and has health issues.?**
>
> **Trade Brandon Jackson for Jason Witten?**
>
> **What are the energy transfers involved in...?**
>
> **Watch One Tree Hill Season 8 Episode 2 I Cant See You But I Know Youre There | Online Video?**
>
> **What dress and jewellery will you gift to your boyfriend who is seriousely getting feminine makeover from now?**

People look to discussion forums to find answers to their questions from average people who are similar to them.

Yahoo! Answers is an example of a very broad discussion forum. There are discussion forums covering almost any specific area. A quick Internet search should show you numerous discussion forums that might host relevant conversations on a given topic. There are discussion boards for technical issues, politics, religion, health, beauty, photography, parenthood and almost any other topic that you can imagine.

Opportunity for Brands

The main opportunity that discussion forums present for brands is the ability to listen to unfiltered conversations and to participate (authentically) in the conversations that are taking place.

This can achieve multiple business objectives. First, it shows that the brand is an active and committed member of the community, which builds trust and positive equity. Second, it can directly drive sales when the community and discussion thread are targeted correctly.

When working at the photography startup, we found a number of photographer discussion forums. We participated in a few general discussions, but I primarily looked for discussions about how to sell and make money from your photography, since that was our business model. By sharing advice and occasionally mentioning our product, we acquired a number of new customers and built awareness for our brand. What made these customers especially valuable is that many of them were actively engaged in a number of discussion forums, so they started mentioning us and recommending us.

Responding to Discussion Forums

The opportunity for businesses here is to find discussion topics that are relevant to their business and offer helpful answers. For example, I recently did a keynote presentation to a group of companies that make over-the-counter pharmaceutical and health care products. I did a quick search in the "injuries" category and found a number of questions on a wide variety of topics.

To leverage the discussion forum, a community manager for Painkiller Brand X could participate in the forums and offer advice. For example, the question "What to do if hit in the face with volleyball?" could be responded to with "Ouch. That must hurt. Ice is generally a great way to prevent swelling, but you probably should consult with your doctor. Hope you feel better! - Tom at Painkiller Brand X"

There are 6 principles to keep in mind when responding to discussion forums.

1. Respond to the topic that is being asked. The most important thing to keep in mind is to respond to the actual question that is asked. Provide a useful response – even if you are only directing them to additional resources.

2. Don't overtly sell. Unless the question is asking for a recommendation for your product or service, don't overtly sell your product. You can build more goodwill and positive equity by being helpful than by selling.

3. If you aren't an expert, be a resource. If you can't directly answer the question, either for legal reasons or because you aren't sure of the answer, you can still participate by being a resource. Post a link to an article or website that has information on the subject being discussed.

4. Play nice. Remember to observe the rules and norms of the community. Keep your participation light and don't get pulled into negative discussions. Even if the discussion is negative about your business or gets personal with you, stay above the negativity.

5. Don't be a spammer. Don't spam or post a standard message on a number of discussion threads. This will probably get you banned from the forum and could embarrass you or your business. Keep your conversations authentic and genuine and stay on topic.

6. Don't fake it. Some businesses want to create "fake" posts when they see a negative discussion about their business. For example, if the discussion says "Brand X Sucks" and a number of people have shared their bad experiences, businesses often want to create fake accounts and leave positive comments to offset the negative. This generally isn't very effective. First, it is typically extremely obvious that the comments left by the business are not authentic. This is a quick way to lose trust. Second, a carefully crafted response could add more value. People complain because they want to be heard and acknowledged. Listen to them. Acknowledge the problem, apologize and tell them what you are going to do about it. This can turn the entire conversation around instantly.

User Reviews & Ratings

User reviews can show up as star ratings for your business on various rating sites, as comments left in a discussion forum, on listings sites like Google Local or Yelp, or as comments left around the web.

User ratings and reviews impact purchase decisions. Research shows that consumers are willing to pay more for a 5-star rated product than a 4-star product. Studies also show consumers are skeptical of overly positive reviews and a few slightly negative reviews can boost overall consumer trust more than strictly positive reviews.

Responding to Ratings and Reviews

It is important for businesses to monitor their reviews and ratings on websites so they can respond as appropriate. Not all review sites give businesses the opportunity to respond, but many do. When responding it is important to directly address the issue and provide a clear action plan. Oftentimes this can turn the discussion around completely.

For example, a client showed me a review where someone had posted that they were treated badly because their coupon was unfairly rejected. The business owner responded and apologized for the bad experience, and stressed that it is never acceptable for his business to treat customers poorly. He went on to say that the coupon in question was actually expired, and to be fair to all customers they have a policy of not accepting expired coupons. The person who originally left the comment actually left an additional comment saying that they had a bad day and understood why the coupon was rejected. If the brand had not responded, only the negative comment would have remained.

Reviews are also helpful in uncovering issues that you might not be aware of with your business. A local coffee shop discovered this when they found negative reviews about their business on Yelp. The reviews commented that while the coffee and atmosphere were great, it was simply too loud. The owner was surprised – there were many reviews about the sound level, but nobody had ever complained to the baristas (probably because they didn't think that it was a fixable problem). The café installed noise absorption panels, the sound level improved and the comments they receive are now primarily positive. If they hadn't looked at review sites they would have continued to lose customers.

When responding to comments on the Internet, it is important to remember that 90% of people will never participate in a discussion or leave a comment, 9% are in-frequent contributors and only 1% contribute regularly. When responding to comments it is important to think about the 99% who will read the interaction but not participate. Even if you can't change the perception of the person who left the rating or review, sharing your side in an objective way can make a difference for the 99% who read it.

Creating Your Own Discussion & Review Forums

In addition to leveraging existing discussion, rating, and review sites, it may be useful to incorporate them on your own existing site. There are a number of pitfalls to beware of if this is a strategy that you are looking to employ.

Discussion Forums

Discussion forums are an extremely popular addition to many websites. From a technical perspective it is relatively easy to add discussion forums onto your website. The bigger question is whether or not you have a passionate and active enough community to support them. Like creating your own social network, launching discussion forums can be like throwing a party where nobody shows up. Prior to launching discussion forums on your site, consider whether there is an active need or desire – are your customers requesting it?

On-site discussion forums can be very valuable – especially for technical products where people may have many questions. For example, the company that hosts my website has discussion forums where I can see technical issues that other users have had as well as different solutions. Many of the questions in the forums are not areas that customer support would normally cover – it is people helping people. Discussion forums can increase engagement levels with your business and lead to more loyalty and sales.

The downside of discussion forums is when there isn't really enough activity to support them. I have seen many businesses add discussion functionality to their websites only to see them left empty. To participate in a discussion forum, users typically have to create an account and sign it – which means that they must have a real reason to want to participate. Consider whether or not this need exists prior to creating discussion forums.

Ratings and Reviews

Ratings and reviews are generally helpful for businesses that have physical products or are selling online. Ratings and reviews are among the biggest factors that ultimately lead to purchase decisions. People trust unbiased opinions from people like them. It can make the difference when someone is on the fence.

The key to successfully incorporating ratings and reviews on your site is to make it clear that the reviews are authentic and not edited. This means that negative reviews are included as well as positive. If negative reviews are not included you will ultimately lose trust.

Including ratings and reviews can make the difference in helping a consumer to ultimately make a purchase, but they must be open and transparent. Share the policy on how the reviews are moderated or edited.

Companies like Bazaar Voice (www.bazaarvoice.com) have software that incorporates ratings and reviews into corporate websites. The software is easy to use and the ratings are authentic. Using a service like Bazaar Voice can help your brand build trust by showing that you are not afraid of what your customers have to say.

Grow Your Reviews Online

Reviews are one of the top factors that influence purchase decisions. Build a strategy to gain positive reviews from your customers on sites like Google and Yelp. Building up positive reviews online proactively means that one customer with a bad experience who gives you a one star review will be overshadowed by positive posts from happy customers.

One quick tip – don't try to create fake reviews or ask your family or friends to review your product online. Most review sites can easily spot and delete fake reviews.

Discussion and review technologies are increasingly included on other social media and Internet platforms. For example, a Facebook fan page can be customized to include discussion forums or ratings and reviews. If ratings and reviews are activated, the business has no ability to edit or alter the reviews. Google also incorporates ratings and reviews into their Google Local listings and will display search results and their star rating. LinkedIn has recommendations and can also facilitate discussions through groups.

If your business can benefit from ratings, reviews or discussions, consider how you can leverage your existing social networks or Internet marketing to achieve this. Existing social networks already have built-in audiences and may be a more natural platform to engage versus creating your own assets.

ACTION ITEMS AND KEY LEARNINGS

Want to put the Social Media Field Guide into Action?
Go to www.bootcampdigital.com/actionplanner to
download your FREE Field Guide action planner.

CHAPTER 13:

Social Media Public Relations

- -

One of the areas that has been most transformed by social media is public relations. Public relations used to be about managing relationships with the press and handling crises. Today public relations is more complicated since virtually everyone has an online voice through social media, bloggers are playing an increasingly large role versus traditional media, and companies are now charged with monitoring and responding to comments and discussions in social media.

Everyone Has a Voice in Social Media – The "Press" Is Everyone

One of the biggest changes that social media has created for public relations professionals is that everyone is press. Prior to social media, a handful of journalists with large audiences were the ones to reach for press coverage. Today, millions of bloggers, Tweeters and Facebookers have access to large audiences to help tell your story. In many cases, brands can get better results by focusing their public relations efforts on a handful of niche blogs with targeted audiences versus vying for a write-up in *The New York Times*. Information spread is decentralized online, and one or two key influencers can start discussion topics that are eventually picked up by *The Wall Street Journal*.

This means that rather than focusing public relations outreach efforts on a handful of reporters, press releases are now being created for the masses via social media.

The Consumer-Focused Press Release

Since regular consumers with social media audiences can now be considered the press, we have seen the emergence of the consumer-focused press release. Rather than writing press releases in a standard, stuffy, boring format, press releases are increasingly consumer-focused.

The content of consumer-focused press releases is more authentic and transparent than traditional press releases. The aim is to tell a story that a blogger or tweeter might be interested in versus adhering to a standard format.

Creating a consumer-focused press release can lead to pick-up for an article by bloggers or mentions on Facebook or Twitter. They key is to create a press release that is interesting to an average consumer and that tells an interesting and engaging story.

The Social Media Press Release

Since "journalists" can be much more broadly defined and social media is playing a bigger role in public relations campaigns, we have seen the emergence of the social media press release.

Pitch Engine (www.pitchengine.com) is the most notable social media public relations distribution site. Rather than posting a traditional press release with standard text, Pitch Engine makes press releases simple to digest and social media friendly.

There are a number of features that differentiate a social media press release versus a traditional press release. First, the content can be summarized in a few short bullet points. Rather than expecting readers to look through the entire press release, the key takeaways are included in a bullet format. Second, multi-media is included, like photos and videos to support the overall story so bloggers can use them in their posts. Third, links are included with descriptions of the links to provide resources to support the story. Finally, the release is summarized into a tweet with a 140-character description of the release.

The social media press release makes for an easier and more efficient way to view and syndicate news announcements. As social media usage increases with journalists and as citizen journalism continues to grow, these will likely increase.

Influencer Outreach

A trend that has been emerging over the years is for brands to do "influencer outreach." The idea is that influencers online can have a large audience that trusts them. By working with influencers, brands can reach their target audience in a highly relevant way with an endorsement from a trusted influencer.

Entire business models and websites are built around this concept. For example, Klout (www.Klout.com) scores users based on their online influence. Brands can work with Klout to send free products to people based on how influential they are and what topics they are influential on.

While Klout offers a scalable way for large organizations to find and connect with large groups of influencers, many small and medium businesses cannot afford a large-scale intiative.

Connecting with influencers is still a huge opportunity for any business or organization. The local symphony in Cincinnati ran a program where they gave away "Tweet Seats." These were free tickets to influencers on Twitter in return for talking about their brand. This increased their visibility with the community, plus helped them build goodwill with people of influence in the comminuty.

Leveraging Bloggers

Leveraging bloggers with highly targeted audiences that trust them is one of the key ways that brands are growing awareness online. Unlike traditional press, bloggers often cover very specific topics and can reach a highly focused audience. There are 5 priary approaches to reaching bloggers:

1. Pitching bloggers like the press

There have been a number of different approaches to blogger outreach. The first is to treat bloggers like traditional press. Find bloggers that target your audience and pitch them to write about you. This is typically the least effective method of blogger outreach.

Again, bloggers don't answer to a boss – they write about what they like. Sure, you think that your product is the greatest thing since sliced bread, but if a blogger doesn't like it or doesn't feel compelled to learn about it, they probably won't cover it. These types of pitches are usually just ignored and deleted, but in worst-case scenarios the blogger may feel annoyed or offended by your pitch and turn against you.

A few years ago I read a blog post from a blogger who was Jewish and was offended that a company pitched her something about Easter, since she doesn't celebrate Easter. In reading the post I was surprised – the blog wasn't about being Jewish, I didn't know she was Jewish (although it was posted on the about page), and certainly most of her readers probably were not Jewish. She was so offended by the PR pitch that she publicly flamed the company for their lack of sensitivity.

In traditional PR, this wouldn't be an issue – even if the writer was Jewish it probably would not impact the stories that are covered; the audience would. In blogger outreach, there is an expectation that pitches are personal and understand the blogger.

Remember, in many cases, a blog is a personal expression outlet, not a billboard. Tread lightly if using this approach and remember that the results probably won't be great.

2. Engage your existing advocates

Engaging and connecting with bloggers who have already mentioned you is another approach to blogger outreach. Rather than finding bloggers who may have an appropriate target audience, finding bloggers who have already mentioned something positive about your company, business or industry can be a much better approach.

The reason that this works well is that you are connecting to bloggers who already have an interest. Rather than connecting with a blogger who may not know or care about your product, connecting with existing enthusiasts can increase their enthusiasm and turn them into advocates.

For example, a few years ago I attended an exclusive blogger party in Las Vegas. One of the sponsors was Love Sac, a company that makes beanbag chairs (really comfortable and giant ones). After the party, I wrote a blog post and I included a photo of me on a Love Sac and mentioned how badly I wanted one. A few days later, a representative from the PR agency for Love Sac emailed me and offered to send me one free. I was ecstatic! I posted about it on Twitter, Facebook and on my blog. Between all of these channels about 30 different people commented back and asked for more information. In addition to reaching my network, the message reached the networks of my friends who also commented on it. The reason that this approach worked so well is that I was already enthusiastic about their product. They also didn't specifically have to ask for something back (this probably would have cheapened the relationship). I naturally wanted to talk about it because I was so excited.

A few weeks later, I saw a blog post about another chair company that tried this in a different way. They found a group of "influencers" in the business community and offered to send them a free chair (their chairs retailed for about $800) in return for a blog post. The email opened with "I know that you don't normally talk about chairs on your blog, but…." This effort was a flop, and a number of bloggers publicly attacked the company for using this approach. Some bloggers even said that a post on their blog was worth more than an $800 chair. I'm sure that some bloggers probably did the single blog post and nothing more. The key is that by pitching bloggers with irrelevant topics, even when you give them something for free, you won't get the same effect as genuine enthusiasm.

3. Build relationships

One of the most effective approaches to blogger outreach is to actually build real relationships with bloggers. This is one of the most effective approaches because it is authentic and actually fosters a long-term relationship that can be leveraged again and again over time.

Building relationships with bloggers takes time and effort. The first step is to identify the bloggers in your target audience that have a large audience you want to leverage. From there, building the relationship can be as simple as becoming friends – starting conversations, interacting and getting to know the person – or as systematic as creating a blogger program.

A number of large companies have created official blogger relationship programs. Wal-Mart has created a blogger network called 11 Moms (although there are now 30) who are influential moms. Wal-Mart compensates them in some fashion (free products, gift cards and connecting them with business opportunities) and the bloggers advocate for Wal-Mart. This official relationship is mutually beneficial to each party.

When I ran marketing for the photography start-up, we created a blogger board of influential bloggers across our target audiences. Our board became enthusiasts and advocates for our company and we gave them formal recognition, publicity and a few small perks. The bloggers helped to promote our product and weighed in on decisions.

One note to consider: there are guidelines from the FTC for disclosures and accuracy of statements when bloggers are compensated financially or with free product. Be sure to research these prior to engaging in these types of arrangements.

4. Give them free stuff

Another option is to offer bloggers free stuff in return for blog posts. This can take many different forms – review samples in return for a review post, free product to run a contest and giveaways for their blog, etc. There are also sites where you can buy reviews from bloggers. Bloggers are paid in return for writing a review post.

This can work, but in many cases it is questionable how authentic the reviews are when compensation is involved. In addition, many of the biggest bloggers require significant compensation and won't write a review for a free bag of chips.

With FTC guidelines surrounding disclosures by bloggers when they are compensated you should do research if you are considering this strategy.

5. Run special programs

Running special blogger programs is another way to build relationships with bloggers and gain mentions in social media. Special programs can include sponsoring parties in conjunction with a blogger conference or hosting blogger days or blogger events.

Many companies including Procter and Gamble, Frito Lay and Johnson & Johnson have hosted blogger days. Invited bloggers attend an all-expense paid trip to learn about the brand or product and share their feedback. There are usually a number of perks involved in these trips. These can be successful as the start of a lasting relationship with bloggers, but on their own they may not create the biggest impact.

Companies have also started to host parties or special events for bloggers and influencers. Last year, Verizon in Cincinnati hosted a party for bloggers when they announced the launch of a new line of phones. They allowed the bloggers to play with the phones and actually use one for a few weeks, free of charge. This was effective in generating buzz and excitement around their new product. The key is to generate genuine enthusiasm rather than requiring bloggers to write in return for free product.

Monitoring and Responding

Businesses can also build equity in social media by monitoring and responding to comments mentioning their business or their industry. Public relations departments are often charged with monitoring and responding to bloggers. This can be a very effective strategy to minimize negativity and super-charge enthusiasts and advocates.

Monitoring Social Media

The first step is to monitor the blogosphere for mentions of your company, brand or industry. Monitoring is an important first step – if you don't know what people are saying about you, you won't be able to respond. Monitoring is an absolutely vital step to getting started in social media marketing.

Depending on the size of your business, this could be a large or small effort. Some large companies have control rooms staffed by multiple people to monitor and respond. Smaller companies may only get a handful of mentions a week, which are much easier to handle.

There are a number of tools to help monitor social media sites for keywords (like your business name, your competitors, your industry or other keywords). The free tools take more time since you need multiple tools for different sites. You can perform a search on Twitter at www.search.twitter. com. Alternatively, you can use a third-party Twitter tool like Hootsuite or Tweetdeck to be notified when keywords are mentioned. With Google Alerts (www.alerts.google.com), you can be notified when your keywords are used in blogs or on the web. These are the free ways to monitor the social web.

There are also a variety of paid tools for social media monitoring, including Trackur (www.trackur.com), Radian 6 (www.radian6.com) or Nielsen (www.nielsen.com). These tools will search across the web including discussion forums, Twitter, blogs, news sites, etc., and find and categorize mentions of your brand. These tools are a great way to streamline your monitoring of social media.

Responding to Social Media Mentions

Bloggers and podcasters like to talk about brands that they love (and hate). Over 80% of bloggers talk about brands they love and hate. Recommendations from friends (which includes social media friends) are a key trusted resource for consumers when deciding what to buy. Showing that your business cares about your customers – whether showing gratitude for a happy customer or showing concern with a dissatisfied one – when responding can build equity and drive sales for your business. If bloggers are speaking about your brand, you should be participating.

Some of the reasons to monitor and participate in the blogosphere include:

- Thank loyal customers for mentioning you.

- Build credibility as an expert or thought leader in your industry.

- Correct misinformation about your brand.

- Solve customer problems.

- Build relationships with your target audience.

- Establish yourself as a thought leader.

- Connect with industry leaders.

- Uncensored and unfiltered focus groups.

When a blogger mentions you, your competitors or your industry, you have an opportunity to join in the conversation.

If you choose to participate and comment, you want to be cautious and do it with tact. The Cluetrain Manifesto[15] advises marketers, "You're invited, but it's our world. Take your shoes off at the door. If you want to barter with us get down off that camel!"

When you enter a blog, you are entering a conversation – often a very personal conversation. It is important that you respect *what the conversation is actually about* and participate in that conversation. If the conversation is about your brand, then by all means, leave a comment specifically discussing your brand. If the conversation is about a subject related to your brand, stick to that subject. Don't be "that guy" by making the conversation all about you.

MARKETING EXAMPLE –
Responding to a Blog Post

I was working with a client who sent me a link to a blog post where a blogger who normally uses their product wrote a mostly positive review about a competitive product.

Let's say the product is soup. The blogger, who normally uses (and likes) soup X, wrote a mostly positive review of soup Y and talked in great detail about the flavors they liked and why. By the time Brand X sent me the blog post, there were about 15 comments, in which different commenters talked about the flavor of soup that they like (e.g., "I love chicken noodle, but tomato is gross"). Brand X wanted to leave a comment supporting their brand and talking about why it was better or worse, even suggested leaving an *anonymous* comment endorsing their brand. The problem was that the conversation wasn't about their brand – it was about soup flavors. The discussion wasn't about their brand.

After discussing the situation we decided to respond in two ways. First, we left a comment on the blog from our brand community manager that was relevant to the conversation "Blogger X - You aren't alone! Did you know that 40% of people also prefer chicken soup over tomato? Also, (random fact) 30% of people say that mushroom soup makes them feel better when they are sick!" This simple comment demonstrated a few things about the brand. First, the brand was listening and engaged in the community (without trying to sell, sell, sell). Second, the brand had knowledge and expertise on soup preferences of consumers. Finally, it gave the brand visibility in the community.

The second action taken by the brand was to write an email to the blogger. The email was brief and personable. It thanked the blogger for mentioning them and related to their love of soup. They also offered the blogger the opportunity to be the first to try (before it was even in stores!) a new flavor. The blogger was surprised and proud that the brand followed their blog and was thrilled to be an insider, and has continued to develop a relationship with the brand.

This was a much more positive and meaningful result than if the brand had simply said "Great post on soup. We hope you still want to try our brand. Did you know that we have 10 vitamins and less sodium than the other brand that you reviewed?" or worse, if they left a comment "I can't believe that you like brand Y – they are terrible. I only use brand X." Neither of these comments would have contributed to the conversation that was actually taking place. The brand would have seemed self-serving and not genuinely interested in the conversation that was happening.

In addition to responding to comments directly about your brand or category, it can be helpful to know, understand and build relationships with key influencers in your category. To get on the radar of key influencers, you can check if they have a blog and leave comments.

Principles for Success When Responding on Social Media

Be cautious when responding to user reviews online – it is important to be transparent and authentic when responding to reviews. Readers of reviews are cynical and look for signals that companies are writing overly positive reviews about their own products or overly negative reviews about competitor products "disguised" as an average consumer.

Be authentic

Be open, authentic and genuine when responding or engaging with social media. Most attempts to "anonymously" post as a "customer" with overly positive comments are completely transparent and actually build distrust. Respond in an authentic and open way to the issue – whether it is positive or negative.

I had a client who had a negative blog post written about their product. Their initial reaction was to post comments from fake people saying that their product was actually great and this blogger was an idiot. Instead, I encouraged them to respond directly and authentically to the blogger. The CEO left a comment, said that he was really concerned that the blogger had a bad experience and that he wasn't satisfied with this problem. He offered to personally look in to it and help solve the problem. This turned the blogger around. The blogger was shocked that the company was listening and that the CEO was going to help solve the problem. After the issue was resolved, the blogger wrote a glowing review about the company.

Respond directly to the issue or subject

Talk directly about what the issue or subject is. Don't dance around the issue – face it head on. Explain you aren't happy about what they experienced and you will try to fix it. Clearly articulate why their coupon was not accepted and why you have that policy. Thank them for the kind words about your company.

Always be direct and straightforward in your responses. Tiptoeing around touchy subjects won't get you anywhere. If you have a policy, be prepared to explain it in a direct way.

Know when to walk away

Just like that song – you gotta know when to fold 'em, know when to walk away and know when to run. Sometimes you can't convert people. There are people out there who like to complain or feel passionately about something and aren't interested in your site.

After explaining your position, don't continue to engage. I had a client that was constantly attacked by PETA (People for the Ethical Treatment of Animals) on their social media sites. Regardless of what the company said about their animal testing policies, the PETA supporters were not satisfied. My client explained their side and then stopped engaging. It is important to share your story even if you aren't going to convert the person who left the comment. I mentioned earlier that only 1% of people regularly create content online –the rest just look at it. Share your side of the story for the 99% who will not actively participate but want to see your side.

Take off your sales hat

You don't have to always be selling. When participating online, leave the marketing lingo at home. Be honest and talk like a real person. Don't sell the people who are already sold.

I'm on the advisory board of a start-up and the CEO recently emailed me because he was excited that he received his first unsolicited blog post. The post was a glowing review of his product. The first thing that I noticed was that he hadn't responded, so I suggested that he respond to the article. He opened by thanking the blogger and then followed it up with 2 -3 marketing sentences. It made the thank-you sound cheap; as though he was really only commenting to further market his product. A better approach would have been a simple thank you, a few kind words and an offer for the blogger to contact you if they ever have feedback.

MARKETING EXAMPLE:
Your Customer Service Sucks

One of my clients launched discussion forums for their members. They were really excited because they spent a lot of time developing the forums and seeding them with interesting content.

The day of the launch I received a panicked phone call. The most popular discussion topic was titled "Your Customer Service Sucks" and it had LOTS of comments. I asked the CEO, "Well, does your customer service suck?" He said yes. It was their biggest priority and they were making major changes. He said that they hear this from customers all the time – including in blog posts.

Rather than deleting the thread, the CEO addressed the issue directly. In a few bullet points, he said that he wasn't happy with the level of customer service either and he outlined the plan to correct it along with specific dates. This totally changed the tone of the discussion. Most people complain to be heard and to get action. Since they followed through with their promise of fixing customer service, he was probably able to hang on to some customers that may have otherwise left and gone to a competitor.

MARKETING EXAMPLE:
Participate in the Actual Conversation

I was working with a client and we discussed the importance of them monitoring and responding to mentions of their product online. They forwarded me an article where they responded. The article reviewed four different products and talked about the pros and cons of each one. The first comment on the post was anonymous and said something like "I Love Product 1. It is the best thing I have ever used. It is so awesome." I don't know for sure, but it definitely sounded like someone from Product 1's company wrote that review. The next comment was from my client and it said something like "Product 2 is the best. I use it all the time and it is really great. I would never use anything else, " and it was also left anonymously.

When I looked at the comments, my initial reaction was that both my client and Product 1 are leaving "anonymous" comments promoting their products. The problem is that in both cases it was pretty obvious that the company was leaving these comments. This can actually have a negative impact as it destroys trust in your brand. If your product was really that great, your advocates would be leaving those comments themselves. If you are willing to mislead people in the comments you leave, where else will you mislead people?

A better response would have been "Hi, I'm Joe, CEO of Product 2. Thank you so much for including us in your review – we really appreciate you taking the time to look at our product and share it with your readers. We aim to make the best product possible and are still at the beginning of this journey, so your feedback is extremely helpful. If you or any of your readers have any questions, comments or ideas about our product, please feel free to drop me a line by phone or email. Thanks again. - Joe, CEO Product 2, 555-555-5555 joe@product2.com." This type of a response would create positive equity for the brand and go much further than anonymous positive product comments.

ACTION ITEMS AND KEY LEARNINGS

Want to put the Social Media Field Guide into Action?
Go to www.bootcampdigital.com/actionplanner to
download your FREE Field Guide action planner.

CHAPTER 14:

Mobile Social Networks

- -

Mobile marketing is a relatively new, but quickly growing, area of social media marketing. More people use text messaging than email. More people have cell phones than use the Internet. In addition, mobile devices like cell phones are always on and always with us.

As consumers adopt smart phone technologies (phones that are always connected to the web like Blackberry, iPhone and Android) that allow applications to run on them, this area will continue to grow and evolve. We are still at the beginning of understanding how mobile technologies will transform our lives.

A discussion about mobile marketing opportunities could be a book in itself. In sticking with the theme of social media marketing, this section will cover the main opportunities and implications for mobile and social media.

Today there are three key opportunities for marketers to leverage mobile as a part of a social media marketing strategy: mobile-only social networks, social media networks on mobile and branded social networks and apps (short for applications). Mobile devices are key enablers of our social lives, so it makes sense they play a big role in social media as well.

Mobile-Only Social Networks

Mobile social networks are social networks created specifically for mobile devices and are primarily accessed through cell phones or mobile devices. Most mobile social networks leverage geo-location data, or the location of the phone from the GPS, as the core of the social network experience. In this way, they leverage social connections based on where you are located.

Mobile-only social networks are downloaded as apps or applications onto smart phones. They may also have websites, but they are primarily accessed through a mobile phone.

There are a number of different geo-location social networks – Foursquare, Whrrl, Facebook Places and many, many more. As these services continue to emerge, it is likely that one or two will gain market prominence and win out. Since social networks are only useful if your friends are on them, there is only room for one or two primary players. Most of these sites are similar in the core functionality for both the user and the opportunities for marketers, but differ in some of their feature sets. For this section, we will primarily focus on Foursquare, which is the largest of these services.

Geo-location social networks answer the key question "Where are you?" and allow users to "check in" to share their current location with their friends. For example, I might be currently "checked in" on Foursquare to the Coffee Emporium, and people who are my friends on Foursquare can see my location. Essentially, social networks like Foursquare allow you to share where you are and what you are doing with your friends.

In addition to simply posting your current location, Foursquare has built in three additional features (based on game mechanics) to increase user engagement. First, each location can have a Mayor. In reality, being the mayor of a location doesn't mean much beyond bragging rights; however, Foursquare users compete for Mayorship over locations. Whenever you check in to a location you can see who the current mayor is. For example, I am the Mayor of my neighborhood bar – whenever anyone checks in they can see that I am the current mayor.

The second part of the gaming mechanics built in to Foursquare is Badges. Users can earn badges by engaging in certain behaviors. For example, I recently earned the "Don't Stop Believing" badge for checking into three karaoke bars in a month (yikes!). There are a variety of general badges created by Foursquare, but brands can also create custom badges that users can earn. For instance, a shopping magazine has created a badge that can be earned by checking into the stores featured in the magazine.

The third aspect of social gaming built into Foursquare is the Leader Board. Foursquare awards points for different things – checking in, adding a new venue, multiple check-ins, checking in at a new place – and compiles leader boards to track points within your network. Again, the points are not really worth anything, but it is another fun way that Foursquare engages users and keeps them active.

Users of Foursquare check in at locations to gain points, Badges and Mayorships as a fun way of showing their friends where they spend their time.

How Marketers Can Use Location Social Networks

There are a number of opportunities for marketers to participate in geolocation social networks. The opportunities differ between each particular site and are still emerging, but there are some consistent trends. Marketers can reward loyalty by offering a special deal for people who have checked in a certain number of times or for the Mayor of their establishment. Geolocation social networks are also offering couponing opportunities based on location. Since sites like Foursquare know where you are, they can offer you deals for establishments nearby.

I was recently in downtown Cincinnati, and as I went to check in on Foursquare I noticed an icon at the top that said "Special Offers Nearby." I clicked on it and saw that RadioShack, which was in the same building, was offering 10% off if I showed my Foursquare check-in. I didn't even know there was a RadioShack in the building. By posting that offer, RadioShack was able to increase my awareness and possibly cause me to purchase there in the future.

Starbucks also ran a campaign with Foursquare. In a national campaign, the Mayor of Starbucks received $1 off a frappacino. When checking in at Starbucks a notification that there was a mayor special appeared. This caused further battles for mayorship since an actual incentive was given to the mayor. Starbucks is able to reward their most loyal customers while increasing awareness. Many hotels offer bonus loyalty points for checking in as well as fitness centers, restaurants and retailers.

If your business has a physical location, encouraging customers to check in has a number of benefits. Customers are broadcasting their location to their social network. This increases brand awareness and loyalty. Location-based social networks are still small, but they are projected to grow as adoption of smart phones increases. Facebook launched Facebook Places, which has similar functionality to Foursquare. Since Facebook already has mass adoption, this will likely accelerate the adoption of location-based social networks.

Social Networks Go Mobile

In addition to social networks designed specifically for mobile devices, web-based social networks are increasingly being accessed through mobile devices. Rather than accessing Facebook, LinkedIn and Twitter from a computer, many consumers are accessing these sites directly from their phones.

This means that participants in the social networks are always on and always connected. It also makes it easier to post and share content on social networks.

The average person has their phone within arm's reach most of the time. Our phones are always on. The always on and always with us mobile devices allow users to stay connected with their social networks 24/7. Consumers can check social networks more than ever before through their phones.

The other implication of social networks on mobile devices is how easy it is to share and post content. In only a few seconds, I can take a picture on my smart phone and with the click of a button post it to Twitter or Facebook. I can tweet or update my Facebook status directly from my phone. Mobile makes it easy to share video and photos at the click of a button – no connecting and uploading to a computer.

Mobile has made staying up-to-date with social networks extremely simple. If you are using social networks for your business, consider leveraging mobile devices to make it easier to share and upload status updates, photos and videos. When I train businesses on how to stay efficient with social networking and get higher returns for lower time investments, updating from mobile phones is one of the key strategies.

Branded Social Networks

A number of branded social networks are also emerging to leverage mobile devices. A branded social network is a social network created by and for a specific brand. These are relatively difficult to create and need to have a strong value proposition for the user. Most people need a good reason to join a social network when they are on one or more already. When evaluating whether or not to create your own social network, your first choice should be to leverage existing social networks (can you create a Facebook application or a LinkedIn group?) versus creating your own branded social network.

A mobile social network that has a clear benefit for consumers can be extremely powerful. Dunkin Donuts has a mobile application and social network called Dunkin Run (www.dunkinrun.com). Dunkin Run is a social network to streamline the process of collecting multiple orders for a trip to Dunkin Donuts. If you are planning to make a trip to Dunkin Donuts you simply schedule the time for your trip and invite your friends to place their orders. The orders can be completely customized. The orders are then collected on a single list and can be printed or sent to your mobile device. When you get to the store you simply show them the list on your phone. Dunkin Run makes trips to Dunkin Donuts easy.

Creating a new social network can be expensive and time consuming, but it can have great results when it is based on the right strategy.

Stay in Tune with Mobile

As mobile technologies improve, a lot of mobile marketing opportunities are emerging. Social media and mobile devices are only the beginning. A number of different applications are dramatically changing the way consumers find information or experience things.

For example, a popular application called Urban Spoon helps you find a restaurant. If you are looking for a specific type of restaurant in a specific location, using a search engine can be difficult. Urban Spoon categorizes by type of restaurant, neighborhood, rating, popularity or location. You can select restaurants and immediately see the ratings or comments (like which dishes were good or bad). This is dramatically changing the way people search for and find restaurants.

With these new technologies, businesses have the opportunity to leverage mobile to grow their businesses. In addition to social media opportunities, mobile marketing presents big opportunities to businesses of all sizes.

ACTION ITEMS AND KEY LEARNINGS

Want to put the Social Media Field Guide into Action?
Go to www.bootcampdigital.com/actionplanner to
download your FREE Field Guide action planner.

PART 3:

Debrief

CHAPTER 15:

Measuring the Results

- - - - - - - - - - - - - - - - - - - -

After implementing your strategy, it is important to continuously monitor and measure your social media marketing, so that you know what is effective. To stay up-to-date and to increase your returns, you have to adapt your strategy or execution based on what works and what doesn't. This brings us to the final steps in the Social Marketing System – Track, Measure

and Adjust. The final stage of the Social Marketing System is vital to refine and improve your social media marketing.

Social media is still a new form of marketing – there isn't a key to guarantee success. Success mostly comes through trial and error. If you don't measure, you won't know what is working or what isn't working, and you may conclude that social media isn't effective. The key to success is continuous improvement and analysis.

Build with Measurement in Mind

When getting started in social media it is absolutely vital to constantly test and measure your social media efforts. Everything from the content or structure of a tweet to the blog topics that get the most feedback should be measured.

Start by trying different things on each social platform. Try tweeting about different topics or experiment with the way tweets are structured. Look at which tweets get the most retweets, which ones get responses and which links get the most clicks. Try different things and measure the results of each variation. This will help you determine the best content for your strategy.

The key to testing is to build your initial social media approach with testing in mind and then follow through with measurement. For example, in your first two weeks of blogging, try ten different blog posts. Look at the five with the most traffic and comments and the five with the least. What do they have in common? What are the choices that lead to success or failure?

When sending out social messages, try to keep most variables constant while only changing one at a time. For example, an initial Facebook post may ask a question. The next one may take the same content and put it in the form of a statement. Alternatively, you may try questions on different subject areas to find the "hot topic" for your audience. They key is to test and learn.

Many companies jump head first into social media and spend a lot of time, money and effort without ever evaluating and improving their approach. Starting with a strong strategy and best practices will put you on the right path, but continuous evaluation and improvement will make the difference between massive success and average results.

Many of the people who come through my training have already dabbled in social media marketing but aren't getting results. They think that social media doesn't work. It does work. Millions of businesses are getting results. The key to success is a strategic approach and constantly improving your execution over time.

The Difficulty of Measuring Social Media

One of the most important choices is to determine the correct metrics for your social media efforts. Social media is tricky to measure because it often touches so many different aspects of an organization from customer service to public relations to product development to customer research. In this way, it can be tough to boil success or failure down to sales numbers.

Additionally, much of social media is difficult to measure – especially if you don't sell products online.

Take a tweet that says, "I just tried Brand Y makeup and I love it! My lips look awesome!" It is obvious that this is valuable for the business, assuming the tweeter has followers. But how valuable is it? How many sales did it drive? Was it because of our social media efforts or would it have happened anyways?

This is what makes social media difficult to measure. We know that there is business value in it, but how, exactly, can we link that to sales? Some social media advocates will say that it can't be. "Trust me. It just works," they say. Well, that doesn't cut it when you have to sell it back to the big boss, or justify the time you are spending to yourself.

The reality is that not all of social media can be measured. In the next segments, I'll cover what to measure and how to measure it, but keep in mind that not everything can be measured. The best approach to measuring social media is a blend of both the qualitative and the quantitative metrics. Report back the numbers and figures, but also look at the types of comments – do they appear to add business value?

Metrics – Link to Objectives

One of the most important choices you have to make is to determine the correct metrics for your social media efforts. Your social media metrics should link back to the initial goals and objectives outlined in your marketing strategy.

If your marketing goal is to connect with existing customers, then measuring sales from existing customers would be the most relevant metric. If, on the other hand, the goal is customer service, the measure may be a decline in phone calls or the number of problems resolved through social media. The metrics should directly tie back to your marketing goals.

Metrics for social media marketing should also be determined upfront, at the outset of your campaign. Once you know your strategy, your tools and your implementation plan, set out what your measures are. If you work for a bigger company, get alignment to what success looks like and how success will be measured.

The reality is that most social media marketing will have a number of goals and objectives – not just one. Some of the goals may not tie directly back to sales (like customer service). Keep that in mind when measuring and include qualitative support as appropriate. While you can directly measure some aspects of social media marketing, many aspects will be difficult to quantify, so it is important to take a holistic approach to measuring.

Measurement Strategy: Action, Engagement, Business Value

One of the biggest challenges companies face when measuring social media marketing and assessing the business value is measuring the right thing. I can't tell you how many smart marketers brag about the number of followers or fans they have but cannot directly or indirectly tie that back to any actual value for their business. Many companies have lots of fans and followers and are getting 0 value from them.

The key to successful measurement is to go beyond the basic bragging metrics and get to actual business value from social media. It doesn't matter how many followers you have if they don't pay attention to you.

Measuring Action

The most basic form of measurement is to measure action – what are you doing and with what frequency. Many businesses confuse this with actual value or engagement. I recently had a business tell me that their social media consultant suggested that their primary measure should be the frequency with which the business posts updates. Sorry folks, in most cases, just showing up doesn't count for much.

Action metrics can help measure the consistency and performance of your social media team but are not very effective at measuring actual results or linking back to business value.

- Action metrics include things like:
- number and frequency of tweets
- number and frequency of blog posts
- number of participations on discussion forums
- number of comments left on other blogs
- number of LinkedIn interactions

The problem with action metrics is that they don't give any indication of the effectiveness of the social media efforts – they simply show that it is happening. Again, it is good to include action metrics as a part of a balanced measurement approach, but this is the most basic form of measurement.

Measuring Engagement

Engagement is the next level of measurement, and this is the one most frequently confused with actual business value. Engagement measures whether or not people are engaging with your brand on social media.

Engagement is often used as a key indicator for social media marketing success because typically (but not always) engagement is an indicator of business value. Studies show that people who interact with brands online are more likely to purchase from them. Studies also show that the more you see a brand online through social sites (like their tweets or Facebook updates) the more likely you are to recall them or to have purchase intent (the intent to buy them).

So, engagement metrics are pretty useful because they are indicators for business value, but they don't actually measure business value.

In a training boot camp that I recently ran, a participant asked about whether or not her fan page was effective. She shared some examples of the posts and firmly concluded that the number of interactions (comments and likes) would tell her if it was effective. WRONG. There are plenty of Facebook posts that get many interactions that don't add business value.

Consider this: I recently read a piece of advice from a social media expert who recommends that all businesses post "What are your plans for the weekend?" on Fridays to drive interaction. While this may generate responses, unless your business is related to weekend entertainment this is a pretty pointless question that probably adds no brand value. It doesn't build equity or positive sentiment – it is just pointless noise. In this case, interaction and business results may have no relation.

The example above is extreme – it is an example of content that is off-topic and not strategic and therefore adds no business value. Engagement is only a strong indicator of business value if the content is strategic and targeted to your audience.

Research on television commercials underscores this. Television commercials that are funny but don't have a strong brand association or inclusion are often not successful at driving sales. Think of the super bowl ads. People remember the funny commercials but often have no idea what product they are for. In the 1990s Taco Bell ran commercials featuring a dog saying "Yo Quiero Taco Bell." The ads were extremely popular and the tag line and dog were so memorable that Taco Bell started selling toy dogs. Sales, however, were not growing. When Taco Bell switched back to commercials that featured their food, sales increased. Engagement doesn't always result in sales. The "home run" of successful marketing is when advertising is strategic and engaging.

The same is true of social media. Engagement metrics are only indicators of success if consumers are engaging with content that strategically highlights your brand.

Engagement metrics measure how engaged fans or customers are with your content. Again, these can indicate business value but not always. Engagement metrics may include:

- Number of followers or fans
- Number of replies on Twitter
- Facebook likes or comments
- Comments on a blog post
- Traffic on blog posts
- Direct messages
- Brand mentions online
- Content created by fans
- Referring traffic to your website
- Clicks on links

Measuring Business Value

The ultimate way to know if your social media marketing is working for you is to measure the actual business value (or sales) derived from your social media marketing activities. Depending on your business this can be easy or difficult.

There are a number of ways to measure business value:

- **Sales that come directly from social media sites** – If you sell products online it is relatively easy to measure the amount of sales that come from social media sites. Most analytics software will track this. It is important to remember that most people visit a website 5.6 times before buying something. So looking only at purchases that come directly from social media can be a narrow approach and miss some of the value.

- **Social media promotions** – Running promotions with traceable numbers can indicate the effectiveness of social media promotions in driving sales. For example, a specific social media coupon code or a sales page that is only promoted on Twitter will help measure this.

- **Email subscribers** – If you run a successful email marketing campaign for your business, you know the value of an email subscriber.

For example, if you sell products to your email list, you can determine how valuable an email subscriber is to your business (e.g., 1 in 10 email subscribers buys $50 worth of products). By tracking email subscribers from social media, you can track business value.

- **Where did you hear about us?** – Asking "Where did you hear about us?" to your email opt-in, sales page, or just to your customers will help determine if social media is working. Simply asking people how they heard about your company will help determine if social media is working.

- **Map social media activities to sales** – If you don't sell products online, it can be difficult to measure business value. One way around this is to create a timeline map of social media activity and chart it against sales. Is there a noticeable difference? Can you see a relationship between sales and social media? Is there a correlation between sales before social media and sales after social media?

The key to measuring business value is to seek out creative ways to directly link sales back to social media activities.

Creating a Balanced Social Media Scorecard

The best approach to measurement is to create a balanced scorecard. A balanced scorecard includes the Action, Engagement and Business Value metrics, but also includes qualitative measurements.

It is important to take a holistic approach to measuring social media marketing to properly understand social media effectiveness. For example, if you are getting fewer website referrals from Twitter, it could be caused by fewer tweets (action) or fewer retweets (activity). By looking at all of the data, you will be in the best position to draw conclusions.

In addition to the quantitative metrics, it is helpful to include qualitative measurements as well. As mentioned earlier, a lot of social media activity is obviously valuable but difficult to exactly quantify. How do you track the value from a positive tweet from a customer? Or a testimonial posted on YouTube? Including sample qualitative information can help paint a bigger picture.

After Measuring – Adjust

It is important to not only measure, but also to adjust your campaign based on what you learned. Look at the execution of your social marketing plan to determine how to create more effective content. Social media marketing is a continuous process – constantly look at what works and doesn't work and adjust your efforts.

For example, let's say you find you have high engagement metrics but aren't actually driving business results or sales. That doesn't mean that social media doesn't work at driving sales. It may mean that your content is not related enough to your product or business. Look for opportunities to create more strategic content that encourages users to engage.

Putting It All Together

We've now covered the entire Social Marketing System from start to finish – from listening to improvement. We created our social media map, or basic plan, and considered all of the different directions that the social media field guide can take us in.

When executing a social media marketing strategy it is important to follow the entire plan laid out in the Social Marketing System. Many businesses have seen results by using this exact system through our Boot Camp Digital training programs.

To further help you in turning your plan into action, we've created a downloadable template that0 walks you through the planning steps outlined in this book. Get your free copy at www.BootCampDigital.com/actionplanner.

All that is standing in your way is developing a strategy and taking action!

ACTION ITEMS AND KEY LEARNINGS

Want to put the Social Media Field Guide into Action?
Go to www.bootcampdigital.com/actionplanner to
download your FREE Field Guide action planner.

**Don't forget to download the
FREE Field Guide Action Planner to start putting
the Social Media Field Guide to work at:**

www.bootcampdigital.com/actionplanner

For bulk pricing on the Field Guide, to book Krista to speak at your event, or for consulting rates and services, please email *info@bootcamp-digital.com* or call us at 646-450-2267.

Boot Camp Digital offers a number of additional training products to help get your internet marketing in shape at *www.bootcampdigital.com/training*.

Online Social Media Boot Camp

The Online Social Media Boot Camp lets you learn social media marketing from start to finish at your own pace. It's our most comprehensive program that covers all of the most important social media marketing tools, and how to build a social media marketing plan for your business. Start your path to success at www.bootcampdigital.com/obc

Social Media "Pin Point" Programs

Our "Pin Point Programs" give you focused and targeted training on a specific topic in social media. These 75-minute training programs help you enhance your social media knowledge in specific topics. New Pin Point Programs are added each month, so view our current catalog at http://boot-campdigital.com/short-training-programs/

Social Media "Masters Circle" Membership Program

This was created for professionals that want to continuously improve and stay up to date on social media marketing. This program features a monthly webinar on a specific social media topic, a monthly Q&A call and a monthly review of the latest trends in social media. This is perfect for professionals who are serious about social media marketing. Get all of the details on the Social Media Masters Circle at www.bootcampdigital.com/masters

Krista Neher is an international speaker, author and recognized authority on social media marketing. Krista has deep roots in marketing with 10+ years of marketing experience, including 5+ years at Procter & Gamble. Krista is currently the CEO of Boot Camp Digital, a leading provider of social media training programs. She is a sought after keynote speaker and trainer, consistently traveling around the world to places like India and England to share her knowl-edge. Krista is originally from Toronto, Canada and currently resides in Cincinnati, Ohio.

Krista is also the author of Visual Social Media Marketing: Harnessing Images, Instagram, Infographics and Pinterest to Grow Your Business Online. It was released in early 2013 and is a best-seller in the exploding field of visual social media marketing. Learn more at www.visualsocialmediamarketing.com.

For bulk pricing on the Field Guide, to book Krista to speak at your event, or for consulting rates and services, please email *info@bootcampdigital.com* or call us at 646-450-2267.

(Endnotes)

[1] www.marketingwithmeaning.com

[2] www.twitter.com/jetblue

[3] www.getsatisfaction.com

[4] tbd

[5] www.scotts.com/smg/connect/blogs/bloglanding.jsp

[6] www.hubspot.com/marketing-webinars/

[7] www.blogs.zappos.com/blogs/fashion-culture

[8] http://blogs.zappos.com/blogs/ceo-and-coo-blog/2010/03/11/zappos-com-update-march-11-2010

[9] www.thelongtail.com/

[10] www.cluetrain.com

[11] www.en.wikipedia.org/wiki/blog

[12] www.wordpress.com

[13] www.blogger.com

[14] www.google.com/alerts

[15] www.cluetrain.com

[16] www.facebook.com